Knowledge Graph Mastery

Building Smarter AI with Graph Reasoning and Semantic Models

Gilbert Huie

Copyright Page

Table of Contents

Preface 5

Chapter 1: Introduction to Knowledge Graphs 8

What Are Knowledge Graphs? 8

The Evolution of Data Representation 10

Why Knowledge Graphs Matter in AI 13

Real-World Applications and Case Studies 16

Chapter 2: Understanding Graph Thinking 20

How Knowledge is Structured in Graphs 20

Graph Databases and Relational Databases 25

Types of Graphs 29

Key Graph Algorithms 34

Chapter 3: Semantic Models and Ontologies 39

Understanding Semantics in AI 39

Ontologies, Taxonomies, and Vocabularies 44

RDF, OWL, and Schema Design 50

The Role of Linked Data and Open Data Standards 55

Chapter 4: Designing a Knowledge Graph from Scratch 61

Identifying the Problem and Scope 61

Data Modeling for Knowledge Graphs 66

Common Design Principles and Mistakes in Knowledge Graphs ...71

Chapter 5: Data Integration and Graph Construction 77

Collecting and Structuring Data 77

Entity Linking and Data Enrichment 82

Cleaning, Deduplication, and Graph ETL Pipelines 88

Chapter 6: Graph Databases and Query Languages 94

Overview of Popular Graph Databases 94

Querying Knowledge Graphs..99

Choosing the Right Graph Database 104

Chapter 7: Knowledge Graphs for Machine Learning 109

How Knowledge Graphs Improve AI Models 109

Graph Embeddings and Representation Learning 114

Case Studies 119

Chapter 8: Graph Reasoning and Inference 124

Rule-Based Reasoning and Statistical Reasoning 124

Automated Inference in AI-Driven Systems 129

Reasoning Frameworks and Tools 134

Chapter 9: Natural Language Processing and Knowledge Graphs .. 140

How Knowledge Graphs Enhance Text Processing 140

Named Entity Recognition (NER) and Relation Extraction..........145

Applications in Chatbots and AI Assistants 148

Chapter 10: Enterprise Applications of Knowledge Graphs.............154

AI-Driven Applications of Knowledge Graphs...........................154

Industry Case Studies and Lessons Learned.............................159

Overcoming Challenges in Knowledge Graph Adoption 164

Chapter 11: Scaling and Optimizing Knowledge Graphs 170

Performance Tuning and Scalability Best Practices 170

Handling Large-Scale and Dynamic Knowledge Graphs..............175

Cloud-Based Solutions and Distributed Architectures................ 180

Chapter 12: The Future of AI and Knowledge Graphs..................... 186

Role of Knowledge Graphs in Artificial General Intelligence 186

Emerging Trends 191

Next Decade of AI-Driven Knowledge Systems 196

Conclusion 201

Preface

The world is drowning in data, yet starving for knowledge. Every second, vast amounts of information are generated, but without proper structure and understanding, this data remains untapped potential. Enter **knowledge graphs**—a transformative way to represent, organize, and reason over data, unlocking the full power of artificial intelligence.

This book, **"Knowledge Graph Mastery: Building Smarter AI with Graph Reasoning and Semantic Models,"** is designed to guide you through the journey of **understanding, designing, and implementing knowledge graphs for AI-driven solutions**. Whether you are a researcher, data scientist, AI engineer, or an industry professional, this book will provide you with the foundational principles and practical tools to harness the power of knowledge graphs in your work.

Why This Book?

AI systems today are evolving rapidly, but they often struggle with **contextual understanding, reasoning, and explainability**—critical aspects of truly intelligent systems. Knowledge graphs bridge this gap by embedding structured knowledge into AI models, allowing them to make sense of the world beyond statistical predictions. Leading companies like **Google, Amazon, Microsoft, and IBM** leverage knowledge graphs to power search engines, recommendation systems, and intelligent virtual assistants. However, despite their immense potential, knowledge graphs remain **underutilized and misunderstood** in many AI and enterprise applications.

This book aims to **demystify** knowledge graphs and show how they can revolutionize AI systems. Through **theory, practical applications, and real-world case studies**, you will learn how to build intelligent systems that **think, reason, and make informed decisions**—just as a human expert would.

What You Will Learn

This book is structured to take you from **fundamentals to advanced applications**, covering both conceptual and hands-on aspects of knowledge graphs. You will explore:

The **foundations of knowledge graphs**, including graph databases, ontologies, and semantic models.

How to **design and implement knowledge graphs**, integrating structured and unstructured data.

The role of **graph reasoning and inference** in making AI more explainable and intelligent.

How knowledge graphs enhance **machine learning and natural language processing** applications.

Real-world case studies from industries like **healthcare, finance, and enterprise AI**.

Best practices for **scalability, optimization, and deployment** of knowledge graphs in production environments.

Who Should Read This Book?

This book is for:
AI Engineers & Data Scientists – Looking to enhance AI models with structured knowledge.
Software Developers – Interested in building intelligent applications with graph-based reasoning.
Enterprise Leaders & Decision-Makers – Understanding how knowledge graphs can power AI-driven business solutions.
Researchers & Academics – Exploring cutting-edge AI techniques that incorporate knowledge representation.

How to Use This Book

The book is designed to be **comprehensive yet accessible**, whether you are a beginner or an experienced practitioner. Each chapter builds upon the previous one, but you can also jump to specific sections based on your needs. **Code examples, best practices, and hands-on exercises** will help you implement the concepts in real-world projects.

At the end of this book, you will have the knowledge and confidence to build **powerful AI solutions** powered by knowledge graphs—bringing intelligence, structure, and reasoning to your data-driven applications.

The future of AI is **not just about bigger models and more data**—it's about making AI **smarter, more explainable, and more aligned with human intelligence**. Knowledge graphs provide the **missing piece** in this puzzle. By mastering them, you are taking a **significant step toward the future of AI**.

I invite you to embark on this journey with me. Let's build AI that **not only predicts but understands**.

Happy learning!

Chapter 1: Introduction to Knowledge Graphs

What Are Knowledge Graphs?

A **knowledge graph** is a structured way of representing information where entities—such as people, places, or concepts—are connected by relationships that define how they interact. Unlike traditional databases that store data in tables, knowledge graphs organize information as a network of linked concepts, making it easier for systems to understand context, draw inferences, and improve decision-making.

At the core of a knowledge graph are three key components:

Entities represent real or abstract things, such as a company, a product, or an event.

Relationships define how entities are connected, such as a company *owns* a product or a person *attended* an event.

Attributes provide additional details about entities, such as a product's price, a company's founding date, or a person's profession.

A simple example of a knowledge graph would be:

"Elon Musk is the CEO of Tesla."

"Tesla produces electric vehicles."

"Electric vehicles help reduce carbon emissions."

Each of these statements forms a connection between entities, allowing AI systems to infer new facts. If a system understands that electric vehicles reduce carbon emissions and Tesla produces electric vehicles, it can infer that Tesla contributes to sustainability efforts.

How Knowledge Graphs Differ from Traditional Databases

In a traditional relational database, information is stored in structured tables with rows and columns. Retrieving insights often requires complex queries that join multiple tables together, which can become inefficient as data volume grows. If a company wanted to analyze how its customers interact with different products, it would need to write extensive queries to link customer purchases, product categories, and user feedback from separate tables.

A knowledge graph, in contrast, stores information in a more natural, connected format. Instead of isolating data into separate tables, it represents relationships explicitly, making it easier to traverse and analyze connections between entities. This structure enables systems to retrieve insights quickly and dynamically, without requiring multiple table joins.

For example, a traditional relational database might store customer purchase data in multiple tables:

One table lists customers.

Another table lists products.

A third table links customers to the products they purchased.

Querying how different products relate to each other based on customer purchases requires multiple joins and can be computationally expensive. In a knowledge graph, these relationships are directly stored as connections between entities, allowing for more efficient queries and analysis.

Why Knowledge Graphs Are Important

Knowledge graphs provide several advantages that make them essential for modern AI applications:

Contextual Understanding
Since knowledge graphs explicitly define relationships, they help AI systems interpret the meaning behind data. For example, a search engine powered by a knowledge graph understands that "Tesla" can refer to both a company and a person (Nikola Tesla). By analyzing context, it can provide more relevant search results.

Efficient Data Integration
Information often comes from multiple sources, such as structured databases, unstructured text, and external APIs. Knowledge graphs integrate these

diverse data formats into a single, interconnected model, enabling seamless data unification.

Advanced Reasoning and Inference

By analyzing relationships, knowledge graphs allow AI to infer new insights that are not explicitly stated. If a knowledge graph contains information about medical conditions and treatments, an AI system can suggest potential therapies based on related conditions, even if a direct link was not manually entered.

Improved AI Explainability

Unlike black-box machine learning models, knowledge graphs provide a clear reasoning path for decisions. This transparency is particularly valuable in applications such as legal analysis, finance, and healthcare, where understanding *why* a system reached a conclusion is just as important as the conclusion itself.

Practical Applications of Knowledge Graphs

Knowledge graphs are widely used across different industries. Search engines use them to improve results by linking concepts instead of just matching keywords. E-commerce platforms leverage them to provide smarter product recommendations based on customer behavior. Healthcare organizations apply them to connect medical research, patient records, and treatment guidelines. Financial institutions use them to detect fraud by identifying suspicious relationships between accounts and transactions.

A knowledge graph represents information in a structured, connected format that enhances understanding, reasoning, and decision-making. It overcomes the limitations of traditional databases by explicitly storing relationships, enabling AI systems to analyze complex connections more efficiently. Whether used for search, recommendation engines, fraud detection, or medical research, knowledge graphs provide a more intelligent way to manage and analyze data.

The Evolution of Data Representation

Data has always been central to decision-making, analysis, and innovation. However, the way data is stored, structured, and used has changed significantly over time. From simple records on paper to advanced AI-powered systems, the evolution of data representation has shaped how businesses, governments, and researchers handle information.

Historically, data was stored in physical formats such as ledgers, books, and filing cabinets. This approach was limited by the inability to process information efficiently. As computers became more widespread, organizations began transitioning to digital data storage, which allowed for faster retrieval and improved accuracy. However, early digital systems were rigid, requiring predefined structures that made it difficult to adapt to new types of information.

The Shift to Structured Digital Data

The introduction of relational databases in the 1970s revolutionized how data was stored and accessed. A relational database organizes information into tables with predefined schemas, where data is stored in rows and columns. Each table represents a specific category of information, such as customers, products, or transactions.

Relational databases became the standard for businesses because they provided consistency, accuracy, and a structured way to query data using SQL (Structured Query Language). They were highly effective for transactional applications, such as inventory management, banking, and enterprise resource planning. However, relational databases have limitations when dealing with highly connected or unstructured information. Retrieving relationships between different types of data often requires complex queries that join multiple tables, leading to slower performance as datasets grow.

The Rise of Unstructured and Semi-Structured Data

As technology advanced, organizations began generating and collecting more data than ever before. Websites, social media, emails, and multimedia content introduced large amounts of unstructured data, which does not fit neatly into tables. To address this challenge, NoSQL databases emerged, offering more flexible ways to store and manage different types of data.

NoSQL databases support key-value stores, document stores, column-family stores, and graph databases, each designed for specific use cases. For instance, document databases such as MongoDB store data in JSON-like structures, making it easier to manage dynamic and hierarchical information. These databases enable greater flexibility, allowing organizations to store and retrieve complex objects without predefined schemas.

However, even with the introduction of NoSQL databases, one challenge remained—how to model relationships effectively. Businesses needed a way to represent knowledge that went beyond isolated records and instead captured meaningful connections between entities. This requirement led to the adoption of knowledge graphs, a representation method that organizes data as a network of interlinked concepts.

The Emergence of Knowledge Graphs

A knowledge graph is a data representation model that connects entities and their relationships in a structured way. Unlike relational databases, which require predefined table structures, or NoSQL databases, which optimize for flexibility, knowledge graphs emphasize the **connections between data points**.

By storing information as nodes (entities) and edges (relationships), knowledge graphs allow AI systems to understand context and draw conclusions based on relationships rather than isolated pieces of data. This approach aligns more closely with how humans think and process information. Instead of seeing data as separate records, a knowledge graph treats it as an interconnected web of knowledge.

For example, if an organization wants to analyze customer behavior, a traditional relational database might store customer interactions in multiple tables that require complex queries to join them together. A knowledge graph, on the other hand, naturally represents how a customer interacts with products, services, and other customers. This structure enables more intuitive queries and reasoning capabilities, making knowledge graphs particularly useful for AI applications, recommendation engines, fraud detection, and natural language understanding.

The Future of Data Representation

As AI and machine learning continue to evolve, the need for more advanced data representation models is becoming increasingly clear. Knowledge graphs are now playing a crucial role in enhancing AI's ability to understand and reason about information. They allow organizations to integrate structured and unstructured data, improve search relevance, and provide more accurate insights.

Traditional databases are not disappearing, but they are being used alongside newer approaches that better handle complexity and relationships. Hybrid models that combine relational, NoSQL, and graph-based storage are becoming more common, ensuring that organizations can leverage the strengths of each system.

The evolution of data representation has been driven by the need to store, access, and analyze information more effectively. From early physical records to relational databases, NoSQL storage, and now knowledge graphs, each step has contributed to building systems that not only store data but also understand and apply it in meaningful ways.

Why Knowledge Graphs Matter in AI

Artificial intelligence relies on data to make predictions, recognize patterns, and automate decision-making. However, raw data alone is not enough to create truly intelligent systems. AI must also understand the **meaning** of data, how different concepts relate to each other, and how to draw logical conclusions. Knowledge graphs provide this missing layer of understanding, enabling AI to go beyond pattern recognition and engage in reasoning and inference.

A knowledge graph organizes data as a network of entities and their relationships, rather than treating information as isolated records. This structure allows AI to analyze the **connections** between concepts, rather than just processing data points in isolation. By explicitly representing relationships, knowledge graphs help AI make better decisions, improve explainability, and integrate knowledge from multiple sources.

Enhancing AI with Context and Meaning

Traditional AI models, particularly those based on machine learning, rely on statistical methods to make predictions. These models learn from large datasets but often struggle with understanding context. For example, a machine learning model trained to recommend books might recognize that users who read a certain genre are likely to be interested in similar books, but it may not understand why those books are related.

A knowledge graph provides this missing context by explicitly defining relationships between books, authors, genres, and historical influences. Instead of merely suggesting books based on similarity scores, an AI system powered by a knowledge graph can explain recommendations, such as suggesting a book because it shares thematic elements with another or because the author was influenced by a writer the user enjoys. This level of reasoning improves AI's ability to provide relevant, insightful responses.

Improving Explainability in AI

One of the biggest challenges in AI is explainability. Many machine learning models function as black boxes, producing results without a clear explanation of how decisions were made. This lack of transparency can be a problem in high-stakes applications such as healthcare, finance, and legal systems, where trust and accountability are critical.

Knowledge graphs address this issue by maintaining a structured representation of knowledge that AI can use to trace the reasoning behind its conclusions. If an AI system recommends a medical treatment, for example, a knowledge graph can show how the recommendation is linked to clinical studies, expert guidelines, and patient history. This transparency makes AI systems more reliable and easier to audit, ensuring that decisions are based on logical and evidence-supported reasoning.

Integrating Data from Multiple Sources

AI applications often need to process information from various sources, such as structured databases, unstructured text, and real-time sensor data. Merging these different types of information into a unified system can be complex, especially when different datasets use different terminologies and formats.

A knowledge graph provides a way to integrate and harmonize data from diverse sources by mapping entities and relationships in a common framework. This enables AI to connect seemingly unrelated information, uncover hidden patterns, and generate insights that would not be possible with separate datasets. For example, in financial fraud detection, a knowledge graph can link transaction data with public records, social networks, and behavioral patterns to identify suspicious activities that might not be obvious through individual data sources alone.

Facilitating Advanced Reasoning and Inference

Beyond storing information, knowledge graphs allow AI to **infer** new facts based on existing relationships. If a knowledge graph contains information about how different drugs interact with specific diseases, AI can use this data to suggest potential treatments for related conditions. This type of reasoning is particularly useful in areas like drug discovery, where AI can identify promising research directions by analyzing existing scientific knowledge.

Inference in knowledge graphs is made possible through logical rules and reasoning techniques. AI can apply rules such as "If a company acquires another company, it also acquires its subsidiaries," allowing it to deduce new relationships automatically. This capability extends AI beyond simple pattern recognition, allowing it to make logical conclusions based on structured knowledge.

Enhancing Natural Language Processing

Natural language processing (NLP) is another area where knowledge graphs significantly improve AI performance. Traditional NLP models often rely on statistical methods to process text, but they may misinterpret meaning when words have multiple meanings. For example, the word "Apple" could refer to the fruit or the technology company, and a machine learning model without contextual understanding may struggle to differentiate between them.

A knowledge graph helps AI resolve these ambiguities by linking words to their meanings in specific contexts. If an AI system encounters the phrase "Apple released a new iPhone," it can use a knowledge graph to recognize that "Apple" refers to the company, not the fruit. This contextual understanding enhances NLP applications such as chatbots, search engines, and document analysis by enabling them to generate more accurate and meaningful responses.

Real-World Impact of Knowledge Graphs in AI

Major technology companies already rely on knowledge graphs to enhance AI capabilities. Google uses a knowledge graph to improve search results by understanding the relationships between people, places, and things. Instead of simply matching keywords, Google can interpret user queries based on known connections, providing more relevant answers.

In e-commerce, platforms like Amazon use knowledge graphs to refine product recommendations by linking customer behavior with product attributes and reviews. This helps AI make more personalized suggestions, improving user experience and increasing sales.

In healthcare, AI-powered knowledge graphs assist doctors by aggregating medical research, clinical guidelines, and patient data to provide evidence-based recommendations. This improves diagnostic accuracy and ensures that healthcare professionals have access to the most relevant information when making treatment decisions.

AI systems need more than just raw data to function effectively. They require structured knowledge that allows them to understand relationships, reason about information, and provide explanations for their decisions. Knowledge graphs enable AI to move beyond simple pattern recognition, adding layers of **context, meaning, and inference** that improve decision-making and reliability.

By integrating knowledge graphs into AI systems, organizations can build smarter applications that offer clearer insights, better user experiences, and more trustworthy outcomes. As AI continues to advance, knowledge graphs will play an increasingly important role in shaping the next generation of intelligent technologies.

Real-World Applications and Case Studies

Knowledge graphs have become an essential tool for many industries, enabling organizations to connect information, uncover insights, and enhance artificial intelligence applications. Their ability to represent relationships between data points makes them particularly useful in areas that require contextual understanding, advanced reasoning, and seamless integration of information from different sources.

One of the most well-known applications of knowledge graphs is in search engines. Google introduced its Knowledge Graph in 2012 to improve search results by understanding the relationships between concepts rather than relying solely on keyword matching. When a user searches for "Leonardo da Vinci," the system does not just return a list of websites containing the name. Instead, it displays a structured summary with key facts about da Vinci, such as his birth and death dates, famous works, and related figures from history. This enhancement allows users to receive more relevant information quickly, and it helps AI better interpret user queries.

In healthcare, knowledge graphs are being used to improve diagnostics, drug discovery, and patient care. Medical research generates vast amounts of data, including clinical trials, scientific papers, patient records, and genetic information. Traditional databases struggle to connect this information in a meaningful way, but knowledge graphs provide a structured representation of medical knowledge. They can link diseases to symptoms, treatments, medications, and patient histories, allowing AI-powered systems to assist doctors in diagnosing conditions and recommending treatments based on related cases. Researchers also use knowledge graphs to identify potential drug interactions and discover new applications for existing medications by analyzing relationships between chemical compounds and biological pathways.

The financial industry relies on knowledge graphs for fraud detection, risk assessment, and regulatory compliance. Financial transactions generate complex networks of interactions between customers, businesses, and financial institutions. A fraudulent transaction is often not obvious when viewed in isolation, but when connected to other transactions and entities, patterns begin to emerge. A knowledge graph can help detect fraudulent activity by mapping relationships between accounts, identifying unusual connections, and flagging suspicious transactions based on past fraud cases. This approach allows financial institutions to respond to threats more effectively and reduce the risk of financial crime.

In e-commerce and recommendation systems, knowledge graphs improve personalization by connecting customer preferences, product attributes, and behavioral data. When a user shops online, traditional recommendation systems often suggest products based on simple patterns, such as items frequently bought together. Knowledge graphs enhance this process by analyzing deeper relationships, such as how a product's features align with a customer's past purchases, search history, and reviews. For example, if a customer frequently buys books on astrophysics, a knowledge graph can recognize related topics, such as quantum mechanics, and suggest books that other users with similar interests have found relevant. This method makes recommendations more meaningful and increases user engagement.

In the legal sector, law firms and regulatory bodies use knowledge graphs to analyze legal documents, case law, and compliance regulations. Laws are interconnected, and a single regulation can have implications across multiple areas. A knowledge graph enables AI to link related legal concepts, identify relevant precedents, and suggest legal arguments based on similar past cases. Lawyers and compliance officers can use these insights to improve legal research, streamline contract analysis, and ensure that businesses adhere to regulatory requirements.

Large enterprises use knowledge graphs to manage corporate knowledge and improve decision-making. Organizations generate vast amounts of internal documents, reports, and project data, often spread across different departments and systems. A knowledge graph consolidates this information by linking related documents, employees, projects, and expertise areas. This allows employees to quickly find relevant information, understand dependencies between projects, and leverage institutional knowledge more effectively. AI-powered assistants built on knowledge graphs can answer company-specific questions, recommend best practices, and facilitate collaboration across teams.

Media and entertainment companies benefit from knowledge graphs by improving content discovery and audience engagement. Streaming services use them to recommend movies and TV shows by analyzing how actors, directors, genres, and viewer preferences are connected. If a user enjoys films by a particular director, a knowledge graph can suggest other works by that director or films that share similar themes and artistic styles. News organizations also use knowledge graphs to categorize articles, link related stories, and provide richer context for readers. When a major event occurs, AI can use a knowledge graph to compile background information, related historical events, and expert opinions, allowing journalists to present more comprehensive coverage.

Knowledge graphs also play a role in cybersecurity, where they help organizations detect threats and prevent attacks. Cyber threats often involve complex networks of actors, compromised systems, and malicious behaviors. A knowledge graph allows security analysts to visualize how different threats are connected, track suspicious activities, and identify vulnerabilities before they are exploited. By mapping relationships between network activity, user behavior, and known threat patterns, AI-powered cybersecurity systems can detect potential attacks more accurately and respond more effectively.

The applications of knowledge graphs continue to expand as more industries recognize their ability to improve AI systems, enhance decision-making, and connect data in meaningful ways. Whether in search engines, healthcare, finance, e-commerce, legal analysis, enterprise knowledge management, media, or cybersecurity, knowledge graphs provide a structured approach to organizing and interpreting information, making AI-powered systems more intelligent, efficient, and reliable.

Chapter 2: Understanding Graph Thinking

Artificial intelligence, data science, and modern analytics are all fundamentally concerned with relationships—how pieces of information connect to each other and what those connections reveal. While traditional databases store data in rows and columns, a **graph-based approach** structures data as a network of interconnected entities. This method of thinking about data, often called **graph thinking**, is what makes knowledge graphs so powerful. Instead of seeing information as isolated points, graph thinking focuses on how those points relate to one another, allowing AI systems to infer new insights and draw logical connections.

To understand why knowledge graphs are so effective, it's important to explore how data is structured in graphs, how they differ from relational databases, and the types of graphs and algorithms that power them.

How Knowledge is Structured in Graphs

When working with data, the way information is structured determines how efficiently it can be accessed, analyzed, and used for intelligent decision-making. Traditional databases arrange data in tables, which are useful for storing well-defined records but struggle when relationships between data points become complex. A graph-based structure takes a different approach by representing data as a network of connected entities, making relationships as important as the entities themselves. This method allows systems to navigate information dynamically, understand context, and infer new insights—capabilities that are essential for modern AI applications.

A **graph** is made up of **nodes** (also called vertices) and **edges** (connections between nodes). Each node represents an entity, such as a person, a product, or a concept, while edges define how these entities relate to each other. This approach mimics how humans naturally connect information in their minds. When reading an article about a historical figure, for example, it is not just about the person but also about their influences, achievements, and connections to other figures. A graph models this interconnectedness explicitly, enabling AI systems to retrieve information in a way that feels more natural and meaningful.

In a knowledge graph, additional information is stored as **properties** associated with nodes and edges. These properties enrich the data model by adding details that refine the meaning of entities and relationships. A graph representing a network of cities, for instance, would not just connect "New York" to "Los Angeles" but would also include information about the distance between them, the available transportation methods, and the estimated travel time. This structure allows systems to perform powerful queries such as "Find the fastest route between two cities" or "Identify cities that serve as major transportation hubs."

Graph-based structures are particularly valuable in AI-driven applications, where context and relationships play a crucial role. In healthcare, a graph can link symptoms, diseases, and treatments, enabling AI to suggest personalized medical recommendations. In finance, fraud detection systems can trace suspicious transactions through interconnected accounts, revealing hidden patterns that would be difficult to identify in a traditional table-based database. By structuring data as a graph, AI systems can move beyond static records and engage in dynamic reasoning.

Graph Model Representation in Code

To better understand how data is structured in a graph, let's build a simple example using Python and the Neo4j graph database. Neo4j is widely used for storing and querying graph data efficiently.

First, install the `neo4j` Python driver if it is not already installed:

```
pip install neo4j
```

Now, let's create a simple graph that represents relationships between people:

```
from neo4j import GraphDatabase

# Connect to Neo4j
uri = "bolt://localhost:7687"  # Change this to
your database URI
username = "neo4j"
password = "password"

driver = GraphDatabase.driver(uri, auth=(username,
password))
```

```
# Function to create people and relationships
def create_graph(tx):
    tx.run("CREATE (:Person {name: 'Alice'})-
[:KNOWS]->(:Person {name: 'Bob'})")
    tx.run("CREATE (:Person {name: 'Bob'})-
[:WORKS_AT]->(:Company {name: 'TechCorp'})")
    tx.run("CREATE (:Person {name: 'Charlie'})-
[:KNOWS]->(:Person {name: 'Alice'})")

# Execute the transaction
with driver.session() as session:
    session.write_transaction(create_graph)

print("Graph created successfully!")
```

This code creates a small graph where:

Alice knows Bob.

Bob works at TechCorp.

Charlie knows Alice.

Once this graph is in place, querying the relationships becomes effortless. For example, to find out where Bob works, you can run:

```
def find_bobs_workplace(tx):
    result = tx.run("MATCH (p:Person {name:
'Bob'})-[:WORKS_AT]->(c:Company) RETURN c.name")
    for record in result:
        print(f"Bob works at {record['c.name']}")

with driver.session() as session:
    session.read_transaction(find_bobs_workplace)
```

Instead of performing multiple table joins, the query simply **traverses the relationships** stored in the graph. This is what makes graph-based systems so powerful.

Comparison with Traditional Databases

In a relational database, the same data would be stored in separate tables:

Person Table

ID Name

1 Alice

2 Bob

3 Charlie

Company Table

ID Name

1 TechCorp

Relationships Table

Person_ID	Relationship	Target_ID
1	KNOWS	2
2	WORKS_AT	1
3	KNOWS	1

Retrieving Bob's workplace would require **joining multiple tables**. In contrast, a graph database retrieves the same information through a direct **relationship traversal**, which is significantly faster and more scalable as the dataset grows.

Real-World Example: Social Networks

Social networks operate on graph-based structures because relationships between users are at the core of how these platforms function. When Facebook suggests "People You May Know," it is analyzing **second-degree connections**—people who are connected to your friends but not directly to you.

A simplified version of this logic in a graph query might look like this:

```
def suggest_friends(tx, person_name):
    query = """
```

```
    MATCH (p:Person {name: $name})-[:KNOWS]-
(friend)-[:KNOWS]-(suggestion)
    WHERE NOT (p)-[:KNOWS]-(suggestion)
    RETURN suggestion.name
    """

    result = tx.run(query, name=person_name)
    for record in result:
        print(f"Suggested friend for {person_name}:
{record['suggestion.name']}")

with driver.session() as session:
    session.read_transaction(suggest_friends,
"Alice")
```

This query follows a **two-hop relationship** to find people who are indirectly connected to Alice but not yet her friends, which is the fundamental logic behind social networking recommendations.

AI and Knowledge Graphs: Beyond Storage

Graph-based systems are not just a way to store data efficiently—they actively **enhance AI reasoning**. Consider a medical diagnosis system that links symptoms to diseases and diseases to treatments. If a patient presents with a set of symptoms, an AI system can use a knowledge graph to identify possible conditions and recommend treatments based on previous successful cases.

For instance, if a knowledge graph contains these relationships:

"Fever" is a symptom of "Flu"

"Cough" is a symptom of "Flu"

"Flu" is treated with "Antiviral Medication"

A simple query can identify that a patient with fever and cough is likely to have the flu and suggest an antiviral treatment. This structured reasoning is difficult to achieve with relational databases, which are not designed to navigate connected knowledge efficiently.

Graph thinking fundamentally changes how data is structured, retrieved, and analyzed. Unlike traditional databases that rely on rigid tables and complex joins, graphs store relationships **natively**, making queries faster, more flexible, and more intuitive. In AI applications, knowledge graphs provide a structured way to enhance reasoning, improve recommendations, and uncover hidden insights by **analyzing connections rather than isolated data points**.

Understanding how knowledge is structured in graphs is essential for building intelligent systems that can navigate and interpret complex information. Whether applied in social networks, healthcare, finance, or AI-driven search, graph-based models unlock new possibilities for data-driven insights and decision-making.

Graph Databases and Relational Databases

Data is everywhere, but how it is stored, accessed, and structured significantly impacts how useful it is. For decades, relational databases have been the standard for organizing data, offering a structured way to store information in rows and columns. While this approach has served businesses well, it struggles with handling complex relationships efficiently.

Graph databases, on the other hand, are designed specifically for working with connected data. Instead of forcing relationships into tables that require complex joins to retrieve meaningful insights, graph databases treat relationships as **first-class citizens**. This approach allows for faster queries, more natural data modeling, and more flexible schemas.

Understanding the differences between these two database models is crucial for anyone working with modern applications, especially as artificial intelligence, social networks, recommendation systems, and fraud detection increasingly rely on relationship-driven data.

How Relational Databases Store and Query Data

A relational database organizes information into tables, with each row representing a record and each column storing an attribute of that record. Tables are linked using **primary keys** and **foreign keys**, which help establish relationships between different pieces of data.

For example, consider a simple e-commerce database that tracks customers and their purchases. There would typically be at least two tables:

Customers Table:

Customer_ID	Name	Email
1	Alice	alice@email.com
2	Bob	bob@email.com

Orders Table:

Order_ID	Customer_ID	Product	Price
101	1	Laptop	$1000
102	2	Smartphone	$700

The **Customer_ID** in the Orders table serves as a foreign key linking it to the Customers table. If we wanted to find out which products Alice has purchased, we would need to join these two tables using an SQL query:

```
SELECT Customers.Name, Orders.Product, Orders.Price
FROM Customers
JOIN Orders ON Customers.Customer_ID =
Orders.Customer_ID
WHERE Customers.Name = 'Alice';
```

This approach works well for structured data where relationships are relatively simple. However, as the number of relationships increases—especially in scenarios such as social networks, fraud detection, or recommendation engines—the need for multiple joins makes queries slow and difficult to manage.

Consider a social media application where users can follow others, like posts, and comment on content. Storing these relationships in a relational database means maintaining multiple tables and performing expensive queries to analyze connections. Finding "mutual friends" between two users, for example, might require several **self-joins**, which can slow down performance significantly as the dataset grows.

How Graph Databases Store and Query Data

A graph database takes a different approach by representing data as **nodes** (entities) and **edges** (relationships between entities). This structure eliminates the need for complex joins by making relationships directly accessible.

Using the same e-commerce example, a graph database would represent Alice, Bob, and their purchases as follows:

Alice → **purchased** → Laptop

Bob → **purchased** → Smartphone

Instead of storing data in separate tables, a graph database keeps everything connected, making queries **faster and more intuitive**.

To retrieve Alice's purchases, a graph database query would look like this in **Cypher**, the query language used by Neo4j:

```
MATCH (customer:Customer {name: 'Alice'})-
[:PURCHASED]->(product)
RETURN product.name, product.price;
```

This query does not require joining tables; instead, it **traverses the relationships** directly, making it significantly more efficient for highly connected data.

Graph databases allow relationships to have **properties**, just like nodes. For example, a **PURCHASED** relationship could store additional details, such as the purchase date or quantity:

```
CREATE (alice:Customer {name: 'Alice'})
CREATE (laptop:Product {name: 'Laptop', price:
1000})
CREATE (alice)-[:PURCHASED {date: '2023-08-15',
quantity: 1}]->(laptop);
```

This model enables deeper insights without requiring complex queries. A single traversal can answer questions such as:

"Which other customers have purchased laptops?"

"What products do Alice and Bob both own?"

"What are the most commonly purchased items?"

This flexibility makes graph databases ideal for use cases where relationships between entities play a central role.

Performance Considerations: Why Graph Databases Excel with Relationships

One of the biggest drawbacks of relational databases is their reliance on **joins** to establish relationships between tables. As datasets grow, joins become more computationally expensive, making queries slower.

For example, consider a fraud detection system analyzing financial transactions. If a fraudster creates multiple accounts and transfers money between them, the system needs to detect suspicious transactions by analyzing relationships between accounts. In a relational database, this requires multiple joins across transaction records, accounts, and customer profiles.

In a graph database, this same problem is handled through a simple **graph traversal**, making fraud detection queries significantly faster. A fraud detection query might look like this in Cypher:

```
MATCH (account1)-[:TRANSFERRED_TO]->(account2)-
[:TRANSFERRED_TO]->(account3)
WHERE account1.balance < 100 AND account3.balance >
10000
RETURN account1, account3;
```

This approach identifies fraudulent activity by tracing **multi-hop connections** between accounts, a process that is significantly more efficient in a graph database than in a relational database.

Real-World Use Cases

Graph databases are widely used in industries where understanding relationships is critical.

In **social networks**, they are used to power friend recommendations, content suggestions, and user interactions. Instead of performing expensive joins to find "people you may know," a graph database efficiently traverses existing relationships to identify common connections.

In **recommendation engines**, graph databases help businesses like Netflix and Amazon suggest movies, products, or services based on user preferences and similar behaviors. By analyzing relationships between users, items, and interactions, recommendations become more accurate.

In **supply chain management**, businesses use graph databases to track relationships between suppliers, manufacturers, distributors, and customers. A company can quickly assess risks by analyzing dependencies in its supply chain, identifying potential bottlenecks before they become major issues.

When to Use Graph Databases Over Relational Databases

Relational databases are still the best choice for applications that require **structured data storage**, **strict consistency**, and **well-defined transactions**, such as banking systems or inventory management.

However, when dealing with **highly connected data**, where relationships play a central role in analysis and decision-making, graph databases provide significant advantages. If an application needs to handle **complex queries that analyze relationships across multiple levels**, such as fraud detection, knowledge graphs, or recommendation engines, a graph database is the better choice.

By understanding the differences between relational and graph databases, developers and data engineers can choose the right tool for the job, ensuring that data is stored, queried, and analyzed in the most efficient way possible.

Types of Graphs

Data is rarely isolated. Whether it's mapping friendships in a social network, tracking the flow of money in financial transactions, or optimizing routes for delivery services, data is connected in ways that reveal deeper insights when relationships are properly structured. The way these relationships are represented determines how efficiently they can be analyzed.

Graphs, as a data structure, provide a natural way to model relationships by representing entities as **nodes (vertices)** and connections as **edges**. However, not all graphs are the same. The type of graph used depends on the nature of relationships, the properties assigned to connections, and the constraints of the system using the graph. Understanding the different types of graphs is crucial for selecting the right structure for a particular application.

Directed vs. Undirected Graphs

One of the most fundamental distinctions in graph structures is whether the relationships have directionality. In some cases, a relationship has a **clear direction**—for example, when one user follows another on social media. In other cases, a relationship is **mutual**, such as friendship connections. This distinction leads to two primary types of graphs:

A **directed graph**, also known as a **digraph**, is a graph where relationships between nodes have a specific direction. Each edge connects one node to another in a one-way manner. If an edge exists from node A to node B, it does not imply that an edge exists from B to A.

For example, in a **Twitter-style** social network, users can follow others without the need for a mutual connection. If Alice follows Bob on Twitter, this does not mean Bob follows Alice back. This relationship can be represented as:

Alice → follows → Bob

The arrow represents the directionality of the relationship, meaning Alice follows Bob, but the reverse is not necessarily true.

To represent this in a graph database such as **Neo4j**, a directed relationship would be stored as follows:

```
CREATE (alice:User {name: 'Alice'})-[:FOLLOWS]-
>(bob:User {name: 'Bob'})
```

A query to find who Alice follows would look like this:

```
MATCH (alice:User {name: 'Alice'})-[:FOLLOWS]-
>(otherUser)
RETURN otherUser.name;
```

This approach makes it easy to answer questions such as:

"Who does Alice follow?"

"Who follows Bob?"

"Which users have the most followers?"

A **directed graph** is useful in situations where relationships are one-way, such as web page linking (where one webpage links to another, but the reverse is not always true), supply chain logistics (where goods move from one supplier to another), and email communications (where one person sends an email to another, but it is not necessarily reciprocated).

In contrast, an **undirected graph** represents relationships where directionality does not matter. If an edge exists between node A and node B, it means both A and B are connected, and there is no concept of one directing the relationship toward the other.

A classic example is a **Facebook-style** friendship model. If Alice and Bob are friends on Facebook, it means the connection is mutual. This can be represented as:

 Alice — friends with — Bob

The absence of an arrow indicates that the connection works both ways.

In Neo4j, an undirected relationship is typically stored using bidirectional edges, meaning two separate relationships would be created—one from Alice to Bob and one from Bob to Alice.

```
CREATE (alice:User {name: 'Alice'})-
[:FRIENDS_WITH]->(bob:User {name: 'Bob'})
CREATE (bob)-[:FRIENDS_WITH]->(alice)
```

An undirected graph works well for situations such as **bi-directional communication networks** (phone calls, real-world friendships, professional connections on LinkedIn), **transportation networks** (where roads allow movement in both directions), and **collaborative projects** (where contributors work together without a strict hierarchy).

Weighted vs. Unweighted Graphs

Another important distinction between graphs is whether the edges have **weights** assigned to them. A **weight** is a numerical value associated with a connection, representing cost, distance, strength, or any other meaningful metric.

A **weighted graph** assigns a value to each relationship, making it possible to represent real-world concepts such as the cost of traveling between cities, the strength of a business partnership, or the similarity between two users based on their preferences.

For example, a **transportation network** can be represented as a weighted graph where cities are nodes and the roads between them are weighted edges based on distance:

New York — (290 miles) — Washington, D.C.

Washington, D.C. — (440 miles) — Atlanta

This means that traveling from New York to Washington, D.C. is 290 miles, while traveling from Washington, D.C. to Atlanta is 440 miles.

In a graph database, this relationship would be stored with a `distance` property:

```
CREATE (ny:City {name: 'New York'})-[:CONNECTED_TO
{distance: 290}]->(dc:City {name: 'Washington
D.C.'})
CREATE (dc)-[:CONNECTED_TO {distance: 440}]-
>(atl:City {name: 'Atlanta'})
```

A query to find all cities reachable from New York along with their distances would be:

```
MATCH (ny:City {name: 'New York'})-
[r:CONNECTED_TO]->(city)
RETURN city.name, r.distance;
```

Weighted graphs are essential in pathfinding problems, where the goal is to find the shortest, fastest, or cheapest route between two points. Algorithms such as **Dijkstra's algorithm** and *A search** use weighted graphs to compute optimal paths in applications like GPS navigation, internet routing, and airline ticket pricing.

In contrast, an **unweighted graph** does not assign any numerical value to relationships. Each connection is treated as equal, meaning there is no concept of "stronger" or "weaker" relationships.

A **social network graph** that simply records friendships without indicating the closeness of the relationships is an example of an unweighted graph. While such a graph can still answer questions like "Who are Alice's friends?" it does not provide insights into which friendships are the strongest or most significant.

Specialized Graph Types: Bipartite, Cyclic, and Trees

In addition to directed, undirected, weighted, and unweighted graphs, some graphs have specialized structures designed for particular applications.

A **bipartite graph** consists of two distinct sets of nodes, where edges only connect nodes from different sets. This is useful in applications such as **job recommendation systems**, where one set represents job seekers and the other represents available jobs.

A **cyclic graph** contains cycles, meaning it is possible to start at a node, follow a sequence of edges, and return to the starting node. **Fraud detection systems** often use cycle detection to identify suspicious financial transactions.

A **tree** is a special type of graph where there is exactly one path between any two nodes. This structure is commonly used in **hierarchical data representations**, such as organizational charts, file systems, and decision trees in AI models.

Choosing the right type of graph structure depends on the relationships within the data and the kinds of queries the system needs to support. Directed graphs are useful when relationships have a defined direction, while undirected graphs are better for mutual connections. Weighted graphs add numerical significance to relationships, enabling applications such as shortest-path calculations and recommendation engines.

Understanding these graph types allows developers, data scientists, and AI engineers to design systems that accurately represent relationships in real-world data. Whether optimizing search algorithms, analyzing social networks, detecting fraud, or improving logistics, the right graph structure ensures that data is not only stored efficiently but also used in a way that generates meaningful insights.

Key Graph Algorithms

When working with graphs, the structure alone is not enough. To extract meaningful insights, navigate relationships efficiently, and make intelligent decisions, we need **graph algorithms**—specialized computational methods designed to analyze and traverse graph structures. These algorithms power applications in social networks, recommendation systems, navigation, fraud detection, and artificial intelligence. They help in finding the shortest paths between locations, detecting influential people in a network, grouping similar data points, and even uncovering hidden patterns in financial transactions.

Understanding these algorithms is essential for anyone working with graph-based data. Whether optimizing a logistics network or building a recommendation engine, choosing the right algorithm makes all the difference in performance and accuracy.

Graph Traversal: Exploring Connections Step by Step

Graph traversal is the process of visiting nodes in a graph in a structured way. Two fundamental traversal techniques are **Breadth-First Search (BFS)** and **Depth-First Search (DFS)**. These are the building blocks of many graph algorithms and help in answering questions such as **"What is the shortest path between two cities?"** or **"How many degrees of separation exist between two people in a network?"**

Breadth-First Search (BFS)

BFS explores all neighbors of a node before moving deeper into the graph. It moves level by level, ensuring that all nodes at the same depth are visited before moving to the next level. This approach makes BFS ideal for **finding the shortest path in an unweighted graph** or **identifying the nearest connections in a social network**.

A classic example is a **friend suggestion system** in a social network. If you want to find people who are two degrees away from you (friends of friends), BFS is the best choice because it first explores all immediate friends before moving to their connections.

Here's a simple BFS implementation in Python using an adjacency list:

```
from collections import deque
```

```
def bfs(graph, start_node):
    visited = set()
    queue = deque([start_node])

    while queue:
        node = queue.popleft()
        if node not in visited:
            print(node, end=" ")   # Process the
node
            visited.add(node)
            queue.extend(graph[node] - visited)

# Sample graph as an adjacency list
graph = {
    'A': {'B', 'C'},
    'B': {'A', 'D', 'E'},
    'C': {'A', 'F', 'G'},
    'D': {'B'},
    'E': {'B'},
    'F': {'C'},
    'G': {'C'}
}

print("BFS Traversal starting from node A:")
bfs(graph, 'A')
```

When run, this prints:

```
BFS Traversal starting from node A:
A B C D E F G
```

Each node is visited in order of increasing distance, making BFS efficient for finding the shortest number of connections between nodes.

Depth-First Search (DFS)

DFS explores as far as possible along one branch before backtracking. It is useful for problems that require **exhaustive searching**, such as finding **all possible paths** between two nodes or detecting **cycles** in a network.

A good example is a **maze solver**. If you're trying to find a way out of a maze, DFS explores one path deeply before trying another, ensuring that all possible routes are considered.

Here's a Python implementation of DFS:

```
def dfs(graph, node, visited=None):
    if visited is None:
        visited = set()
    if node not in visited:
        print(node, end=" ")  # Process the node
        visited.add(node)
        for neighbor in graph[node]:
            dfs(graph, neighbor, visited)

print("\nDFS Traversal starting from node A:")
dfs(graph, 'A')
```

This prints:

```
DFS Traversal starting from node A:
A B D E C F G
```

DFS goes as deep as possible before backtracking, making it useful for applications such as **solving puzzles, detecting cycles in graphs, and checking connectivity**.

Shortest Path Algorithms: Finding the Most Efficient Route

Finding the shortest or most efficient path between two points is a common problem in graphs. Whether optimizing delivery routes, navigating through city streets, or routing network traffic, **shortest path algorithms** play a critical role.

Dijkstra's Algorithm: The Foundation of Navigation Systems

Dijkstra's algorithm finds the shortest path from a starting node to all other nodes in a graph with **non-negative** edge weights. It is widely used in **GPS navigation, airline ticket pricing, and network routing**.

For example, when you use Google Maps to find the quickest way from one city to another, Dijkstra's algorithm calculates the shortest path based on road distances or estimated travel times.

Here's an implementation of Dijkstra's algorithm in Python:

```python
import heapq

def dijkstra(graph, start):
    priority_queue = []
    heapq.heappush(priority_queue, (0, start))
    distances = {node: float('inf') for node in
graph}
    distances[start] = 0

    while priority_queue:
        current_distance, current_node =
heapq.heappop(priority_queue)

        for neighbor, weight in
graph[current_node].items():
            distance = current_distance + weight
            if distance < distances[neighbor]:
                distances[neighbor] = distance
                heapq.heappush(priority_queue,
(distance, neighbor))

    return distances

# Weighted graph representation
weighted_graph = {
    'A': {'B': 1, 'C': 4},
    'B': {'A': 1, 'C': 2, 'D': 5},
    'C': {'A': 4, 'B': 2, 'D': 1},
    'D': {'B': 5, 'C': 1}
}

print("\nShortest distances from node A:")
print(dijkstra(weighted_graph, 'A'))
```

This outputs:

```
Shortest distances from node A:
{'A': 0, 'B': 1, 'C': 3, 'D': 4}
```

Dijkstra's algorithm ensures that the shortest path to any destination is always found first, making it ideal for **real-time navigation and logistics planning**.

37

Centrality Algorithms: Finding the Most Influential Nodes

In many applications, identifying the most influential nodes in a graph is important. **Centrality algorithms** measure how important a node is based on its position in the network.

PageRank: The Algorithm Behind Google Search

PageRank is used to determine the importance of web pages based on the number and quality of links to them. A page that is linked to by many important pages is considered highly important itself. This algorithm powers Google Search, ranking web pages by relevance.

The idea behind PageRank is simple: **If many important pages link to a webpage, it must be important too.**

A basic implementation of PageRank using NetworkX looks like this:

```python
import networkx as nx

# Create a directed graph
G = nx.DiGraph()
edges = [('A', 'B'), ('A', 'C'), ('B', 'C'), ('C',
'A'), ('D', 'C'), ('E', 'C'), ('E', 'D')]
G.add_edges_from(edges)

# Compute PageRank
pagerank_scores = nx.pagerank(G)
print("\nPageRank Scores:")
for node, score in pagerank_scores.items():
    print(f"{node}: {score:.4f}")
```

Nodes with higher scores are considered more influential based on the number and quality of incoming connections.

Graph algorithms are the backbone of intelligent systems that analyze relationships, optimize networks, and uncover hidden insights. Whether searching through social networks, planning routes in navigation systems, or ranking websites in search engines, these algorithms transform raw data into meaningful patterns. By understanding and applying the right algorithm, developers and data scientists can unlock the true power of graph-based data.

Chapter 3: Semantic Models and Ontologies

Data is more than just numbers and text; it carries meaning. When artificial intelligence systems process information, they do more than store facts—they attempt to **understand** relationships, contexts, and concepts. This understanding is what makes AI truly intelligent, enabling it to **reason, infer, and generate meaningful insights**.

To achieve this, AI systems rely on **semantic models**—structured representations of knowledge that define how concepts relate to each other. These models give AI the ability to **interpret data beyond raw words** and understand the meaning behind them.

Imagine an AI system analyzing the phrase:
"Apple releases a new device."

Without semantics, the AI may struggle to determine whether "Apple" refers to a **company** or a **fruit**. A semantic model, however, stores knowledge about "Apple Inc." being associated with "technology," "iPhones," and "products," making it clear that the sentence refers to a **tech company launching a gadget**.

This structured understanding is what **semantic models and ontologies** provide. They form the foundation for **search engines, knowledge graphs, and intelligent assistants**—allowing AI to move beyond keyword matching to real comprehension.

Understanding Semantics in AI

Artificial intelligence processes vast amounts of data every second, but its true power comes not from raw computation alone, but from its ability to **understand meaning**. Without an understanding of semantics, AI remains limited to pattern recognition, treating words and data points as isolated symbols rather than as components of a connected system of meaning.

Semantics in AI refers to the ability of machines to **interpret, infer, and apply meaning to data**. It enables AI to go beyond simple keyword matching and surface-level analysis, allowing it to understand **context, relationships, and intent**. This is what differentiates an advanced AI system—such as a virtual assistant that can understand complex questions—from a basic keyword-based search engine that simply retrieves results based on text similarity.

To appreciate why semantics is crucial in AI, consider a simple sentence:

"The bank approved my loan."

A conventional AI model that relies purely on statistical analysis might struggle with the word **"bank."** Does it refer to a **financial institution**, or is it a **riverbank**? A human can easily determine that the meaning refers to a financial institution based on the surrounding words ("approved" and "loan"). AI needs **semantic understanding** to make this same distinction, ensuring that it interprets language **correctly** rather than relying on word frequencies or simple pattern matching.

How Semantics Transforms AI

When an AI system understands semantics, it does not just process words—it understands **concepts and their relationships**. This ability allows AI to perform tasks that require **reasoning, inference, and contextual awareness**.

For example, if an AI system is analyzing medical reports, it must recognize that:

"Fever" is a symptom of "Influenza."

"Paracetamol" is used to treat "Fever."

If a patient has "Influenza," a possible treatment could be "Paracetamol."

This is not a simple word-matching process. The AI must recognize **hierarchical relationships** and use them to **infer new knowledge**. This structured understanding is essential in fields like healthcare, legal research, and intelligent search engines, where AI systems must process complex and nuanced information.

Semantic AI is also essential in **chatbots and virtual assistants**. If a user asks, **"What's the best laptop for programming?"**, an AI system that understands semantics can interpret the user's **intent** rather than just the individual words.

It can determine that "best" is subjective, "laptop" refers to a category of electronic devices, and "programming" has specific requirements such as **RAM, processing power, and keyboard quality**.

Instead of returning a generic list of laptops, a semantically aware AI could generate a **personalized response**, taking into account factors like user preferences, reviews, and technical specifications.

Challenges in Achieving Semantic Understanding

Teaching AI to understand meaning is challenging because language is **ambiguous, context-dependent, and constantly evolving**. The same word can have different meanings depending on **context**, and meaning itself can be **subjective**.

For instance, if an AI encounters the sentence **"He saw the man with binoculars."**, does this mean:

The **man** had the binoculars?

He (the observer) used binoculars to see the man?

A human can often resolve this ambiguity using context, but for AI, this requires advanced **semantic modeling techniques** that analyze sentence structure, word relationships, and real-world knowledge.

Another major challenge is that human language often involves **implicit knowledge** that is not explicitly stated in text. If someone says **"She didn't bring an umbrella, so she got wet."**, the AI must infer that **it was raining**, even though the sentence does not mention rain directly. These types of logical inferences require AI systems to be built with **knowledge graphs, ontologies, and inference engines** that help them **connect implicit information** and derive conclusions.

Key Approaches to Teaching AI Semantics

Several techniques have been developed to help AI interpret meaning and context. Some of the most important methods include:

1. Word Embeddings and Semantic Vectors

One of the earliest breakthroughs in AI's understanding of semantics was the development of **word embeddings**—mathematical representations of words based on their meanings and relationships. These embeddings allow AI to recognize that words like **"king" and "queen"** are related, even if they do not appear together frequently in training data.

Popular word embedding models such as **Word2Vec, GloVe, and FastText** assign numerical representations to words, positioning similar words **closer together** in a high-dimensional space. This enables AI to recognize **synonyms, analogies, and contextual similarities**.

For example, Word2Vec allows AI to learn:

$$king - man + woman \approx queen$$

This is a form of **semantic reasoning**, where AI can infer relationships between words based on how they are used in language.

A simple implementation of Word2Vec in Python using `gensim` looks like this:

```
from gensim.models import Word2Vec

# Sample sentences
sentences = [
    ["king", "queen", "prince", "princess"],
    ["man", "woman", "boy", "girl"],
    ["apple", "orange", "banana", "fruit"]
]

# Train a simple Word2Vec model
model = Word2Vec(sentences, vector_size=100,
window=5, min_count=1, workers=4)

# Find similar words to "king"
similar_words = model.wv.most_similar("king")
print(similar_words)
```

The model will return words that are **semantically similar** to "king" based on context, helping AI understand relationships between concepts.

2. Knowledge Graphs for Structured Understanding

While word embeddings help AI understand word relationships statistically, **knowledge graphs** provide **explicitly structured relationships** between concepts. A **knowledge graph** organizes information into nodes (concepts) and edges (relationships), allowing AI to traverse **semantic relationships** rather than relying solely on probability.

For example, a knowledge graph might store:

"Tesla" is a "company"

"Elon Musk" is the "CEO" of "Tesla"

"Tesla" produces "electric vehicles"

Using this structured knowledge, AI can answer complex queries such as **"Who is the CEO of the company that makes electric vehicles?"** by reasoning through its **semantic relationships** rather than relying on text pattern matching.

A simple way to create a knowledge graph using **Neo4j** in Python:

```
from neo4j import GraphDatabase

# Connect to the Neo4j database
driver =
GraphDatabase.driver("bolt://localhost:7687",
auth=("neo4j", "password"))

def create_knowledge_graph(tx):
    tx.run("CREATE (:Company {name: 'Tesla'})-
[:CEO]->(:Person {name: 'Elon Musk'})")
    tx.run("CREATE (:Company {name: 'Tesla'})-
[:PRODUCES]->(:Product {name: 'Electric
Vehicle'})")

# Execute the transaction
with driver.session() as session:

session.write_transaction(create_knowledge_graph)

print("Knowledge graph created!")
```

This structured approach enables AI systems to **reason over data**, linking information in a way that mimics human understanding.

3. Semantic Parsing and Natural Language Understanding

Another technique AI uses to process semantics is **semantic parsing**, which converts natural language into a structured format that machines can process. Instead of just identifying keywords, AI systems analyze **sentence structure, dependencies, and logical meaning**.

For example, in a question-answering system, semantic parsing helps break down:

"Which company makes the best electric cars?"

Into structured components:

Subject: Company

Action: Makes

Object: Electric cars

This allows AI to **find the most relevant answer** based on structured meaning rather than word frequency.

Semantics is what allows AI to move beyond basic keyword recognition and develop an **understanding of meaning, relationships, and context**. By integrating **word embeddings, knowledge graphs, and semantic parsing**, AI systems can process information in a way that is closer to human reasoning.

This ability to interpret meaning enables AI to **answer complex questions, improve search accuracy, generate intelligent recommendations, and make informed decisions**. As AI continues to evolve, semantics will remain at the core of building **truly intelligent** systems.

Ontologies, Taxonomies, and Vocabularies

When artificial intelligence processes information, it does not simply store words and phrases—it needs to **understand relationships, hierarchy, and context**. To achieve this, AI systems use structured frameworks that define how concepts relate to each other. These frameworks, known as **ontologies, taxonomies, and vocabularies**, provide the foundation for **knowledge** organization, **search engines, recommendation systems, and natural language understanding**.

Each of these terms represents a **different level of structuring knowledge**. Taxonomies provide a **hierarchical classification**, vocabularies define **agreed-upon terms**, and ontologies establish **rich relationships and reasoning rules** between concepts. Together, they ensure that AI does not just match words but truly understands **the meaning behind them**.

Taxonomies: Structuring Knowledge into a Hierarchy

A taxonomy is a way of **classifying concepts into parent-child relationships**, creating a structured hierarchy where each concept belongs to a broader category. This structure ensures that information is **organized logically** and that AI can infer relationships based on categorization.

For example, in an **e-commerce store**, a taxonomy for products might look like this:

```
Electronics
|— Laptops
|      ├— Gaming Laptops
|      ├— Business Laptops
|— Smartphones
|      ├— Android Phones
|      ├— iPhones
```

In this structure, if a user searches for "Laptops," the system understands that both "Gaming Laptops" and "Business Laptops" are **subcategories**, allowing AI to **return more relevant results**.

Taxonomies are widely used in **e-commerce, content management, and search engines**, where information must be categorized for efficient retrieval.

In AI applications, taxonomies allow systems to:

Suggest related content by recognizing category relationships.

Improve search results by expanding queries to include relevant subcategories.

Enhance recommendation systems by identifying products or services within the same classification.

A simple taxonomy can be stored in a **graph database** like Neo4j. Below is an example of how you might structure a product taxonomy in Neo4j using Cypher:

```
CREATE (:Category {name: "Electronics"})-
[:HAS_SUBCATEGORY]->(:Category {name: "Laptops"})
CREATE (:Category {name: "Laptops"})-
[:HAS_SUBCATEGORY]->(:Category {name: "Gaming
Laptops"})
CREATE (:Category {name: "Laptops"})-
[:HAS_SUBCATEGORY]->(:Category {name: "Business
Laptops"})
```

With this structure in place, a query like:

```
MATCH (c:Category {name: "Electronics"})-
[:HAS_SUBCATEGORY*]->(subcategories)
RETURN subcategories.name
```

Would return all subcategories under "Electronics," allowing AI to navigate and suggest products **intelligently**.

Vocabularies: Standardizing Meaning Across Systems

While taxonomies organize concepts into categories, **vocabularies define the specific terms used within a system**. A vocabulary ensures that different people—or different AI systems—use **consistent terminology** to describe the same concepts.

For example, in **healthcare**, different medical records might refer to "heart attack" using different terms:

"Myocardial infarction" (scientific term)

"MI" (abbreviation)

"Heart attack" (layman's term)

A vocabulary standardizes these variations so that AI understands they refer to the **same medical condition**.

Commonly used vocabularies include:

SNOMED CT (Healthcare) – Standardized medical terminology used in electronic health records.

Schema.org (Web) – A vocabulary that defines structured data for search engines to understand web content.

ISO 4217 (Finance) – Standard currency codes like "USD" for US dollars.

Vocabularies are essential in:

Semantic search, where AI needs to recognize synonyms and related concepts.

Cross-system communication, where AI integrates data from multiple sources with different naming conventions.

Data interoperability, ensuring that information can be shared across different AI applications.

A simple example of storing vocabulary relationships in a graph database:

```
CREATE (:Concept {name: "Heart Attack"})-
[:SYNONYM]->(:Concept {name: "Myocardial
Infarction"})
CREATE (:Concept {name: "Heart Attack"})-
[:SYNONYM]->(:Concept {name: "MI"})
```

A query like:

```
MATCH (:Concept {name: "Heart Attack"})-[:SYNONYM]-
>(synonyms)
RETURN synonyms.name
```

Would return all recognized synonyms, allowing AI to **understand different terms as referring to the same medical condition**.

Ontologies: Establishing Meaning and Relationships

An ontology is more advanced than a taxonomy or vocabulary. It **not only categorizes concepts** but also defines **how they relate to each other and allows AI to infer new knowledge**. Ontologies enable AI to go beyond simple classification and **reason about relationships dynamically**.

For example, in a **legal knowledge system**, an ontology can define:

A "Contract" must have at least one "Party."

A "Party" can be an "Individual" or a "Company."

A "Breach of Contract" occurs if a "Party" fails to fulfill "Obligations."

With this structure, AI can infer that if **"Company X" failed to deliver goods, it is a "Breach of Contract"**, even if that specific scenario was not pre-programmed.

Ontologies are widely used in:

Medical AI, where AI can infer potential diagnoses based on symptom-disease relationships.

Legal AI, where systems can assess contract compliance based on predefined legal structures.

Enterprise AI, where organizations model business processes and rules for automation.

Ontologies are built using standards such as **OWL (Web Ontology Language)**, which enables AI to define relationships and logical constraints.

A basic ontology in OWL might look like this:

```
<Class rdf:ID="Person">
   <subClassOf rdf:resource="#Entity"/>
</Class>

<Class rdf:ID="Company">
   <subClassOf rdf:resource="#Entity"/>
</Class>

<ObjectProperty rdf:ID="employs">
   <domain rdf:resource="#Company"/>
   <range rdf:resource="#Person"/>
```

```
</ObjectProperty>
```

This defines that **"Companies employ People,"** allowing AI to infer that if **"TechCorp employs Alice,"** then Alice is an employee of TechCorp.

Ontologies provide AI with **formalized reasoning capabilities**, enabling it to make intelligent decisions without needing explicitly programmed rules.

How These Concepts Work Together in AI Systems

Taxonomies, vocabularies, and ontologies are not competing approaches—they **work together** to give AI a **rich understanding of data**.

For example, a **medical AI assistant** might use:

A taxonomy to classify diseases into broader categories (e.g., "Influenza" under "Viral Infections").

A vocabulary to recognize different terms for the same condition (e.g., "MI" vs. "Heart Attack").

An ontology to infer that "Chest Pain" as a symptom could indicate "Heart Disease."

By combining these frameworks, AI can **understand, reason, and generate intelligent responses**, rather than simply retrieving text that matches keywords.

Taxonomies, vocabularies, and ontologies form the **backbone of semantic AI**, providing structured meaning to data. A taxonomy organizes concepts into a **hierarchical structure**, a vocabulary standardizes the **terms used**, and an ontology defines **rich relationships and rules** that enable AI to **reason dynamically**.

These frameworks are crucial for **search engines, healthcare AI, legal reasoning, enterprise knowledge management, and recommendation systems**. As AI continues to evolve, its ability to understand and **infer meaning** from structured knowledge will remain one of its most critical capabilities.

RDF, OWL, and Schema Design

Data alone is not enough for artificial intelligence to function intelligently—it must be structured in a way that allows systems to **understand, query, and reason about relationships**. The challenge is that data often comes from multiple sources, in different formats, and with varying levels of complexity. To bring meaning and consistency to data, AI systems rely on **semantic web technologies**, particularly **RDF (Resource Description Framework), OWL (Web Ontology Language), and structured schema design**.

These technologies provide a **universal framework** for describing data and their relationships in a way that both humans and machines can interpret. They allow AI to infer new knowledge, integrate disparate datasets, and make decisions based on **structured, machine-readable semantics**.

Understanding RDF: The Foundation of Semantic Data

At its core, RDF is a **graph-based model** that represents knowledge as a set of **triples**. Each triple consists of:

A subject (an entity being described)

A predicate (a property or relationship)

An object (the value or related entity)

For example, consider this simple statement: *"Elon Musk is the CEO of Tesla."*

In RDF, this would be broken down into:

Subject: Elon Musk

Predicate: is CEO of

Object: Tesla

This allows AI to process data **not as isolated text, but as structured, interconnected knowledge**.

RDF is commonly written in **Turtle (TTL) notation**, a human-readable format for representing triples. The example above would be written as:

```
@prefix ex: <http://example.com/> .

ex:ElonMusk ex:isCEOof ex:Tesla .
```

If you want to provide additional details, such as birthdate and nationality, the RDF graph expands naturally:

```
ex:ElonMusk ex:isCEOof ex:Tesla ;
            ex:birthDate "1971-06-28" ;
            ex:nationality "American" .
```

Each piece of knowledge becomes a **structured relationship** that AI can **query, infer from, and integrate with other datasets**.

Why RDF Matters in AI and Knowledge Graphs

RDF is fundamental to **knowledge graphs, semantic search, and linked data** because it allows different datasets to be **combined and queried** as if they were a single, unified knowledge base.

For instance, if an AI system needs to answer: *"Who is the CEO of the company that manufactures electric vehicles?"*

It can retrieve:

Tesla manufactures electric vehicles.

Elon Musk is the CEO of Tesla.

This kind of structured reasoning is impossible with **unstructured text-based data** alone. RDF makes AI **aware of relationships**, enabling smarter recommendations, decision-making, and search capabilities.

OWL: Adding Intelligence and Reasoning to RDF

While RDF **stores relationships**, OWL **adds logic and reasoning capabilities**, allowing AI to **infer new knowledge** beyond explicitly stated facts.

For example, RDF can tell an AI:

"A Tesla is an Electric Car."

"All Electric Cars are Vehicles."

51

OWL allows the AI to **infer automatically** that:

"A Tesla is a Vehicle."

This ability to **deduce relationships that are not explicitly stated** is critical for **semantic AI, medical diagnosis systems, legal analysis, and recommendation engines**.

Defining Classes and Properties in OWL

OWL extends RDF by allowing entities to be grouped into **classes** with defined relationships. Instead of simply listing facts, OWL lets us **define concepts and rules**.

For instance, in a **medical ontology**, we can define:

A "Disease" class.

A "Symptom" class.

A relationship where diseases have symptoms.

In OWL syntax, this would look like:

```
<Class rdf:ID="Disease"/>
<Class rdf:ID="Symptom"/>
<ObjectProperty rdf:ID="hasSymptom">
    <domain rdf:resource="#Disease"/>
    <range rdf:resource="#Symptom"/>
</ObjectProperty>
```

This defines a **universal rule** that any entity classified as a "Disease" can have a "Symptom".

Now, if we add specific diseases:

```
<NamedIndividual rdf:ID="Influenza">
    <rdf:type rdf:resource="#Disease"/>
    <hasSymptom rdf:resource="#Fever"/>
    <hasSymptom rdf:resource="#Cough"/>
</NamedIndividual>

<NamedIndividual rdf:ID="Fever">
    <rdf:type rdf:resource="#Symptom"/>
```

```
</NamedIndividual>
```

If AI is asked, **"What symptoms does Influenza have?"**, it can now return **"Fever" and "Cough"**, even if it was not explicitly programmed with this knowledge.

OWL Enables Advanced AI Reasoning

Using OWL, AI can:

Infer missing facts. If "Influenza" is a "Disease" and diseases "have symptoms," AI **knows** that **Influenza must have symptoms**.

Enforce consistency. AI can validate that no entity classified as a "Person" is also a "Vehicle."

Answer complex queries. AI can determine that if **a patient has a set of symptoms**, they are likely suffering from **a related disease**.

Schema Design: Structuring AI's Knowledge for Efficient Queries

A well-designed **schema** ensures that AI **retrieves, integrates, and processes** data efficiently. A schema defines **how entities are classified, how they relate to one another, and how constraints are applied**.

For example, in a **financial AI system**, we might need to structure:

Banks (institutions that hold assets).

Accounts (owned by individuals or businesses).

Transactions (moving money between accounts).

Graph Schema in Neo4j

If we are designing a schema in a graph database like Neo4j, we define **nodes and relationships** as:

```
CREATE (:Bank {name: "Chase"})
CREATE (:Person {name: "Alice"})
CREATE (:Account {number: "12345"})
CREATE (:Transaction {id: "T001", amount: 500,
date: "2023-08-01"})
```

```
MATCH (b:Bank {name: "Chase"}), (a:Account {number:
"12345"})
CREATE (b)-[:HAS_ACCOUNT]->(a)

MATCH (p:Person {name: "Alice"}), (a:Account
{number: "12345"})
CREATE (p)-[:OWNS]->(a)

MATCH (a1:Account {number: "12345"}), (a2:Account
{number: "67890"}), (t:Transaction {id: "T001"})
CREATE (a1)-[:SENDS {amount: t.amount, date:
t.date}]->(a2)
```

This schema ensures that AI can efficiently answer:

"Who owns Account 12345?"

"Which transactions occurred on August 1, 2023?"

"What is the relationship between Alice and Chase Bank?"

Ensuring Schema Scalability

A well-designed schema must be:

Flexible (easily accommodate new entities and relationships).

Efficient (optimized for quick traversal and querying).

Consistent (maintain data integrity across systems).

For large-scale AI applications, schemas integrate **RDF and OWL for reasoning**, while databases like Neo4j or SPARQL endpoints handle **real-time querying and data storage**.

AI needs more than just raw data—it requires **structured knowledge** to reason, infer, and answer complex questions. RDF provides a **graph-based data model**, OWL enables **logical reasoning**, and schema design ensures that AI systems can efficiently **store, retrieve, and integrate** information.

These technologies are the foundation for **knowledge graphs, intelligent assistants, semantic search engines, and AI-driven decision systems,** ensuring that AI moves beyond keyword matching to true **understanding and reasoning**.

The Role of Linked Data and Open Data Standards

The internet contains an overwhelming amount of information, but most of it exists in disconnected silos. A government database may store company registrations, a scientific research database may contain medical studies, and a news website may report on business activities. Even though these datasets may reference the same entities—such as a company, a drug, or a public figure—they are often stored in different formats and are not easily connected.

This lack of connectivity limits the usefulness of data. For artificial intelligence systems, knowledge graphs, and data-driven applications to function effectively, they need **structured, interlinked, and machine-readable data** that allows them to **connect different pieces of knowledge** and extract meaningful insights.

This is where **Linked Data and Open Data Standards** come in. These principles and technologies ensure that data is **not only available, but also structured in a way that allows different systems to understand and use it**.

Understanding Linked Data

Linked Data is an approach to publishing and connecting structured data on the web. It ensures that **datasets can reference each other using standard identifiers (URIs) and can be accessed in a machine-readable format**.

At the core of Linked Data is a simple yet powerful principle: **Each entity (a person, place, event, or concept) should have a unique identifier (a URI) that links to other related entities.**

For example, in a traditional database, a company might be identified using an internal ID like `company_id=1234`. This ID means nothing outside that system. However, in a Linked Data environment, the company might have a globally unique identifier like:

```
http://dbpedia.org/resource/Tesla,_Inc.
```

This URL does more than just identify the company—it allows any system to **fetch additional structured information about Tesla, such as its CEO, founding date, headquarters, and related entities**.

To see Linked Data in action, let's look at a **real-world example**.

Example: How Linked Data Powers AI and Knowledge Graphs

A search engine answering the question **"Who is the CEO of Tesla?"** benefits from Linked Data in the following way:

The AI queries a **knowledge graph** that stores structured information about companies and executives.

The graph contains a Linked Data reference to **DBpedia** (a structured version of Wikipedia).

The AI follows the link to DBpedia and retrieves Tesla's structured information.

The CEO property of Tesla is linked to another entity—**Elon Musk**—which provides more relevant information about him, including his nationality, other ventures, and biography.

The result is an **intelligent answer**, not just a list of websites containing the words "Tesla" and "CEO."

This ability to **navigate structured relationships across multiple sources** is what makes Linked Data so powerful.

How Linked Data is Structured: RDF and SPARQL

Linked Data is based on the **Resource Description Framework (RDF)**, which structures information as **triples**:

Subject → The entity being described (e.g., Tesla).

Predicate → The relationship (e.g., has CEO).

Object → The related entity or value (e.g., Elon Musk).

This structure enables AI to understand and query relationships efficiently.

Example: Representing Tesla's CEO in RDF

```
@prefix dbo: <http://dbpedia.org/ontology/> .

@prefix dbr: <http://dbpedia.org/resource/> .
```

```
dbr:Tesla,_Inc. dbo:chiefExecutiveOfficer dbr:Elon_Musk .
```

If an AI system queries **"Who is the CEO of Tesla?"**, it can retrieve this triple and return the answer: **Elon Musk**.

To query RDF data, we use **SPARQL**, a query language designed for Linked Data.

Here's how you would retrieve Tesla's CEO using SPARQL:

```
PREFIX dbo: <http://dbpedia.org/ontology/>
PREFIX dbr: <http://dbpedia.org/resource/>

SELECT ?ceo WHERE {
  dbr:Tesla,_Inc. dbo:chiefExecutiveOfficer ?ceo .
}
```

This query returns **Elon Musk**, making it easy for AI to integrate information dynamically.

The Importance of Open Data Standards

While Linked Data enables structured interconnectivity, **Open Data Standards** ensure that data is **accessible, reusable, and consistent across different platforms**. Without these standards, every organization would define its own format, making interoperability impossible.

What are Open Data Standards?

Open Data Standards define **how** data should be structured and shared to ensure that it can be understood and processed by different systems. These standards allow:

Government agencies to share public records in a format that researchers and AI can process.

Healthcare providers to exchange patient data securely and efficiently.

Search engines to interpret structured data from websites, improving results for users.

Examples of Open Data Standards

Schema.org – A vocabulary that helps web pages structure information so that search engines can understand and index it.

FOAF (Friend of a Friend) – A standard for describing people and social relationships in a structured format.

DCAT (Data Catalog Vocabulary) – Used by governments to publish open data in a machine-readable format.

OpenStreetMap (OSM) – A collaborative geographic data standard used by navigation apps.

Real-World Impact of Open Data Standards

Take **Schema.org**, for example. When a website provides structured data using Schema.org markup, search engines like Google can extract **rich snippets**—enhanced search results with additional information.

A recipe website using Schema.org might include:

```
<script type="application/ld+json">
{
  "@context": "https://schema.org/",
  "@type": "Recipe",
  "name": "Chocolate Cake",
  "author": {
    "@type": "Person",
    "name": "John Doe"
  },
  "cookTime": "PT30M",
  "recipeIngredient": [
    "2 cups flour",
    "1 cup sugar",
    "1/2 cup cocoa powder"
  ]
}
</script>
```

This structured data allows search engines to display rich snippets showing:

Recipe name

Cooking time

Ingredients

Author

Instead of relying on **keyword extraction**, AI **understands** that this is a **recipe** and extracts the key details **intelligently**.

Why Linked Data and Open Data Standards Matter for AI

AI thrives on **structured, interconnected, and standardized** data. Without Linked Data and Open Data Standards, AI would struggle to **connect related concepts, infer new knowledge, and provide meaningful insights**.

Enhancing AI Capabilities

Semantic Search and Smart Assistants

AI assistants like Siri and Google Assistant use **structured knowledge from Linked Data sources** like Wikidata and DBpedia to answer queries accurately.

Fraud Detection and Financial AI

Banks and regulators link transaction data across multiple institutions to detect fraudulent activities. A Linked Data approach ensures that AI can trace financial relationships across different datasets.

Healthcare and Drug Discovery

Medical research benefits from structured datasets that link **clinical trials, drug interactions, and patient records**. AI systems can **connect medical studies worldwide**, accelerating drug discovery.

News and Misinformation Detection

AI models tracking breaking news can **cross-reference multiple data sources** to verify accuracy, helping to combat misinformation.

Linked Data and Open Data Standards form the **foundation of AI-powered knowledge and decision-making**. Linked Data enables AI to **connect disparate datasets into a meaningful network of knowledge**, while Open Data Standards ensure that **information is structured consistently across different systems**.

These principles power **knowledge graphs, search engines, smart assistants, and AI-driven applications**, making AI more accurate, transparent, and insightful. As AI continues to evolve, its ability to **understand and integrate structured, linked knowledge** will be a defining factor in its success.

Chapter 4: Designing a Knowledge Graph from Scratch

Building a knowledge graph is not just about collecting data—it's about **structuring information in a way that AI can understand, reason with, and derive insights from**. A well-designed knowledge graph transforms raw data into a **network of connected knowledge**, allowing AI to answer complex questions, make intelligent recommendations, and provide meaningful interpretations of relationships between concepts.

Designing a knowledge graph from scratch requires a **thoughtful approach**—defining the problem it will solve, modeling the data effectively, and following best practices to ensure scalability and accuracy.

Identifying the Problem and Scope

Building a knowledge graph is not just about connecting data points—it's about **solving a real problem**. Without a well-defined purpose, a knowledge graph can quickly become an overcomplicated structure filled with loosely connected information that fails to deliver real value. The first and most critical step in designing a knowledge graph is to **clearly define the problem it aims to solve and the scope it will cover**.

This step is essential because a knowledge graph is **not just another database**. It is a structured representation of relationships that helps **AI reason, infer new knowledge, and provide intelligent insights**. Designing a knowledge graph without defining the problem and scope leads to **data overload, inefficient queries, and an unclear purpose**.

Every knowledge graph should have a **clearly articulated purpose**. A well-defined problem provides clarity on **what data needs to be included, what relationships should be modeled, and how the graph will be used in practice**.

To define the problem effectively, start by asking:

What kind of knowledge needs to be represented?
A knowledge graph could be built to structure medical knowledge for

disease diagnosis, represent legal relationships between contracts, or store product recommendations for an e-commerce platform.

Who will use this knowledge graph, and how will they interact with it? Will it be used by **AI systems** for automated reasoning, **human analysts** for research, or **search engines** for semantic search?

What kind of questions should the knowledge graph answer? Should it return simple factual relationships (e.g., "Who directed this movie?"), infer hidden insights (e.g., "Which suppliers are at risk of disruption?"), or recommend actions (e.g., "Which financial transactions show patterns of fraud?")?

What external data sources does the knowledge graph need to integrate with?
Will it pull data from **databases, APIs, open knowledge repositories (like Wikidata), or structured datasets (like Schema.org)?**

Real-World Example: Healthcare Knowledge Graph for AI Diagnosis

Let's take a **healthcare use case** to understand this step better. Suppose a hospital wants to build an **AI-powered medical diagnosis assistant**.

The hospital's problem statement might look like this: **"Doctors need a system that can quickly analyze patient symptoms and suggest potential diagnoses along with recommended treatments."**

The scope of the knowledge graph must be clearly defined to ensure that the system delivers **relevant, evidence-based recommendations**.

The graph must contain **medical conditions (diseases), symptoms, and treatments**.

It should capture **the relationships between symptoms and conditions** (e.g., Fever → caused by → Influenza).

It should link **treatments to conditions** (e.g., Paracetamol → treats → Fever).

It should integrate with **external sources like clinical trial databases** for updated treatment guidelines.

By defining the problem this way, the team avoids adding **irrelevant** data like hospital locations, insurance policies, or unrelated medical procedures, keeping the graph **focused and effective**.

Defining the Scope: What to Include and What to Exclude

Scope determines **what should and should not be included** in the knowledge graph. A poorly scoped graph may become too broad, making queries inefficient and difficult to maintain. Conversely, a graph that is too narrow may fail to provide meaningful insights.

To define the scope effectively, break it down into **three key areas**:

1. Core Entities and Relationships

At the heart of a knowledge graph are **entities** (nodes) and **relationships** (edges). Each entity represents a **real-world object**, and each relationship defines how these entities are connected.

In a **fraud detection knowledge graph**, the core entities might include:

Bank accounts

Transactions

Account holders

The relationships might include:

Account A → transfers money to → Account B

Person X → owns → Account A

Transaction Y → flagged as suspicious → by AI model

If the scope is **not clearly defined**, irrelevant data may be introduced, such as the personal spending habits of account holders, which may not contribute to fraud detection.

2. The Depth of Relationships and Inference

Another key decision in scope definition is **how deep the knowledge graph should go in its relationships**.

For example, in a **supply chain knowledge graph**, should it stop at direct suppliers, or should it trace relationships back to **sub-suppliers and manufacturers**?

If the goal is to **identify supply chain risks**, the graph may need to track **multiple layers of relationships**, such as:

Manufacturer → depends on → Raw material supplier

Raw material supplier → located in → Region affected by floods

However, if the goal is **basic inventory tracking**, a shallower graph may be sufficient.

3. Integration with External Datasets

A knowledge graph rarely exists in isolation. It often needs to **ingest data from multiple sources** to enrich its knowledge.

For example, a **legal knowledge graph** used in contract analysis may need to pull data from:

Internal company databases for signed contracts.

Public legal databases for past litigation cases.

Regulatory websites for updated compliance laws.

If these integrations are **not defined upfront**, the knowledge graph may lack **critical context**, reducing its usefulness.

Practical Implementation: Designing a Schema for a Financial Knowledge Graph

Let's say we are designing a **financial knowledge graph** to detect fraud in bank transactions.

Step 1: Define the Core Problem

"Banks need an AI system that detects fraud patterns by analyzing relationships between accounts, transactions, and flagged behaviors."

Step 2: Define the Entities and Relationships

Entities (Nodes):

Accounts (identified by account numbers)

Customers (identified by unique customer IDs)

Transactions (linked to sender and receiver accounts)

Relationships (Edges):

Account → owned by → Customer

Transaction → moves money from → Account A to Account B

Account → flagged as risky → by fraud detection system

Step 3: Implement the Schema in a Graph Database

Using Neo4j, we can define the schema and relationships:

```
CREATE (:Customer {name: "Alice", customer_id:
"C12345"})
CREATE (:Customer {name: "Bob", customer_id:
"C67890"})
CREATE (:Account {account_number: "A001"})
CREATE (:Account {account_number: "A002"})
CREATE (:Transaction {transaction_id: "T001",
amount: 5000, date: "2023-08-01"})

MATCH (c:Customer {customer_id: "C12345"}),
(a:Account {account_number: "A001"})
CREATE (c)-[:OWNS]->(a)

MATCH (c:Customer {customer_id: "C67890"}),
(a:Account {account_number: "A002"})
CREATE (c)-[:OWNS]->(a)

MATCH (a1:Account {account_number: "A001"}),
(a2:Account {account_number: "A002"}),
(t:Transaction {transaction_id: "T001"})
CREATE (a1)-[:SENDS {amount: t.amount, date:
t.date}]->(a2)
```

Step 4: Query the Knowledge Graph

To find **all transactions sent by Alice**, we can run:

```
MATCH (c:Customer {name: "Alice"})-[:OWNS]-
>(a:Account)-[:SENDS]->(t:Transaction)
RETURN t.transaction_id, t.amount, t.date
```

This structured approach ensures that fraud detection AI **can analyze transaction patterns and detect anomalies efficiently**.

A well-defined **problem statement and scope** are essential for designing a knowledge graph that is **useful, efficient, and scalable**. By identifying **core entities, relationships, depth of inference, and external integrations**, we ensure that the graph is **focused on solving a real problem**.

The key to success is **clarity**—the more precisely the problem and scope are defined, the more powerful and effective the knowledge graph will be.

Data Modeling for Knowledge Graphs

Building a knowledge graph is not just about connecting data—it's about structuring information in a way that makes sense to both humans and machines. Data modeling is the process of **defining the entities, relationships, and properties** that will form the foundation of the knowledge graph. A well-structured data model allows AI to **query, reason, and infer new knowledge** efficiently.

When done correctly, data modeling ensures that the knowledge graph is **scalable, maintainable, and optimized for answering complex questions**. Without a strong model, the graph can quickly become disorganized, leading to inefficient queries and a lack of meaningful insights.

At the heart of every knowledge graph are **entities, relationships, and properties**. These elements define how data is structured and how AI can navigate and extract meaningful connections.

Entities (Nodes) and Their Properties

Entities, also known as **nodes**, represent real-world objects, concepts, or abstract ideas. Each entity has properties that describe its characteristics.

For example, in a **medical knowledge graph**, the following entities might exist:

66

Disease (name, description, risk factors)

Symptom (name, severity, frequency)

Medication (name, dosage, side effects)

Each entity carries **structured properties** that define what it represents.

Example: Representing an Entity in Neo4j

```
CREATE (:Disease {name: "Influenza", description:
"A contagious viral infection affecting the
respiratory system."})
CREATE (:Symptom {name: "Fever", severity: "High",
frequency: "Common"})
CREATE (:Medication {name: "Paracetamol", dosage:
"500mg", side_effects: "Nausea, Dizziness"})
```

This structure ensures that AI can **retrieve, filter, and analyze** diseases, symptoms, and medications based on their attributes.

Relationships (Edges) and Their Direction

Relationships define how entities connect. Each relationship has a **type** and may also carry **properties** that provide additional details.

For example, in the same medical knowledge graph:

A disease causes a symptom

A medication treats a disease

A treatment has side effects

Each relationship is **directional**, meaning it points **from one entity to another** to represent meaningful connections.

Example: Creating Relationships in Neo4j

```
MATCH (d:Disease {name: "Influenza"}), (s:Symptom
{name: "Fever"})
CREATE (d)-[:CAUSES]->(s)

MATCH (m:Medication {name: "Paracetamol"}),
(d:Disease {name: "Influenza"})
```

```
CREATE (m)-[:TREATS]->(d)

MATCH (m:Medication {name: "Paracetamol"}),
(se:Symptom {name: "Nausea"})
CREATE (m)-[:HAS_SIDE_EFFECT]->(se)
```

This ensures that AI can **trace relationships between diseases, symptoms, and medications**, enabling **medical diagnosis and treatment recommendations**.

Schema Design for a Scalable Knowledge Graph

A good knowledge graph schema is **designed for performance and flexibility**. It must support:

Efficient queries that can retrieve information with minimal computation.

Scalability so new entities and relationships can be added without breaking existing structures.

Consistency to avoid duplicate or conflicting information.

Let's structure a **financial fraud detection knowledge graph**.

Step 1: Define Entities

A fraud detection system may track:

Customers (name, ID, risk score)

Bank Accounts (account number, balance)

Transactions (amount, timestamp, location)

Step 2: Define Relationships

Customers own bank accounts

Transactions move money between accounts

Suspicious transactions get flagged

Step 3: Implement Schema in Neo4j

```
CREATE (:Customer {name: "Alice", id: "C123",
risk_score: "Low"})
```

```
CREATE (:Customer {name: "Bob", id: "C456",
risk_score: "High"})

CREATE (:Account {account_number: "A001", balance:
10000})
CREATE (:Account {account_number: "A002", balance:
50000})

CREATE (:Transaction {transaction_id: "T001",
amount: 5000, timestamp: "2023-08-01"})

MATCH (c:Customer {id: "C123"}), (a:Account
{account_number: "A001"})
CREATE (c)-[:OWNS]->(a)

MATCH (a1:Account {account_number: "A001"}),
(a2:Account {account_number: "A002"}),
(t:Transaction {transaction_id: "T001"})
CREATE (a1)-[:SENDS {amount: t.amount, timestamp:
t.timestamp}]->(a2)
```

Now, if AI needs to detect suspicious transactions, it can run a **fraud detection query**:

```
MATCH (t:Transaction)-[:SENDS]->(a:Account)
WHERE t.amount > 4000 AND a.balance < 10000
RETURN t.transaction_id, t.amount, a.account_number
```

This query **flags large transactions** involving accounts with **low balances**, helping financial institutions detect fraud patterns.

Best Practices for Knowledge Graph Data Modeling

A well-modeled knowledge graph **improves performance and reasoning capabilities**. Here are key principles to follow:

1. Use Meaningful Relationship Types

Avoid generic relationship names like **"RELATED_TO"**. Instead, use specific terms like **"EMPLOYS"**, **"OWNS"**, or **"TREATS"** to make relationships explicit.

2. Store Critical Information as Properties, Not Separate Nodes

69

If a property is **not an entity**, store it as a **property instead of a separate node**.

Bad practice:

```
CREATE (:Account)-[:HAS_BALANCE]->(:Balance
{amount: 10000})
```

Better approach:

```
CREATE (:Account {account_number: "A001", balance:
10000})
```

This ensures **faster retrieval** without unnecessary complexity.

3. Optimize Query Performance with Indexing

For high-performance queries, index frequently used properties:

```
CREATE INDEX ON :Customer(id)
CREATE INDEX ON :Account(account_number)
```

This speeds up search queries significantly.

4. Avoid Data Duplication

Each entity should exist **only once** in the graph. Instead of creating duplicate customer nodes, reference existing ones in relationships.

For example, before adding a new customer, check if they already exist:

```
MERGE (c:Customer {id: "C123"})
ON CREATE SET c.name = "Alice", c.risk_score =
"Low"
```

This prevents duplicate entries, ensuring **data integrity**.

5. Allow for Future Expansion

A knowledge graph must be **flexible enough to grow**. Instead of hardcoding rigid categories, use a **hierarchical structure**.

For example, instead of:

```
CREATE (:Disease {name: "Influenza"})
CREATE (:Disease {name: "COVID-19"})
```

Use:

```
CREATE (:Disease {name: "Influenza"})-
[:SUBCLASS_OF]->(:Category {name: "Viral
Infections"})
CREATE (:Disease {name: "COVID-19"})-
[:SUBCLASS_OF]->(:Category {name: "Viral
Infections"})
```

This allows **new diseases to be added under the same category**, ensuring **future compatibility**.

Data modeling is the foundation of an **effective and scalable knowledge graph**. By structuring entities, relationships, and properties correctly, AI can efficiently **store, retrieve, and infer knowledge**.

A well-modeled knowledge graph ensures that:

Data is stored efficiently

Queries return insights quickly

The structure is scalable and future-proof

Whether designing a **medical diagnosis system, a financial fraud detector, or a recommendation engine**, the **right data model** is the key to unlocking the full potential of AI-powered reasoning and decision-making.

Common Design Principles and Mistakes in Knowledge Graphs

Building a knowledge graph is not just about linking data points—it's about **structuring knowledge in a way that makes sense, scales efficiently, and serves a meaningful purpose**. The way data is modeled impacts the performance of queries, the accuracy of AI-driven reasoning, and the overall usefulness of the graph.

When a knowledge graph is designed well, it provides **clear relationships between entities, efficient data retrieval, and the ability to infer new insights**. However, when design mistakes creep in, they lead to **slow performance, redundant data, inconsistent relationships, and ultimately, an unusable graph**.

The best knowledge graphs share a few common characteristics: **clarity, efficiency, consistency, and adaptability**. The design should enable both **AI reasoning and human interpretability**, ensuring that the graph structure remains logical and easy to query.

1. Define Clear and Meaningful Relationships

Every connection in a knowledge graph must **mean something specific**. A common mistake is using **generic relationship types**, such as `"RELATED_TO"`, which do not provide enough meaning for AI to process relationships correctly.

Instead, relationships should be **explicit and semantically meaningful**. If the graph represents **a company's structure**, instead of using:

```
CREATE (:Person {name: "Alice"})-[:RELATED_TO]-
>(:Company {name: "TechCorp"})
```

It should use a **clear relationship**:

```
CREATE (:Person {name: "Alice"})-[:WORKS_FOR]-
>(:Company {name: "TechCorp"})
```

Now, when AI queries **"Who works for TechCorp?"**, it can retrieve **accurate and meaningful results**.

2. Optimize for Query Performance

A poorly designed knowledge graph leads to slow queries, especially when handling large datasets. Performance issues typically arise when:

The graph has **too many redundant relationships**, leading to unnecessary complexity.

Queries require **deep traversal** due to improper indexing or relationship structures.

To optimize performance, relationships should be **structured in a way that minimizes traversal depth**.

For example, in a **fraud detection system**, if an account is involved in a suspicious transaction, AI should be able to quickly **trace connections** without unnecessary complexity.

```
MATCH (a:Account {account_number: "A001"})-
[:SENDS]->(t:Transaction)-[:TO]->(b:Account)
RETURN a, t, b
```

If accounts are linked through multiple unnecessary intermediate nodes, queries become **slow and inefficient**.

Indexing frequently queried properties also **improves performance**. If the system often searches for **customer IDs**, an index should be created:

```
CREATE INDEX ON :Customer(id)
```

This ensures that lookups happen **instantly instead of scanning the entire graph**.

3. Avoid Redundant Data and Duplicate Entities

One of the most common mistakes in knowledge graph design is **duplicating entities**. When the same entity appears multiple times, it leads to inconsistencies, incorrect query results, and wasted storage.

For example, if a knowledge graph contains multiple instances of the same person:

```
CREATE (:Person {name: "Alice", email:
"alice@email.com"})
CREATE (:Person {name: "Alice", email:
"alice@email.com"})
```

An AI system trying to analyze Alice's transactions **may not recognize that these two nodes represent the same person**.

To prevent this issue, use **MERGE** instead of **CREATE**, ensuring that duplicate entities are not created:

```
MERGE (p:Person {email: "alice@email.com"})
ON CREATE SET p.name = "Alice"
```

This guarantees that Alice is **only stored once**, preventing inconsistencies in data retrieval.

4. Model Data Based on Query Use Cases

A well-designed knowledge graph must be optimized for the **questions it needs to answer**. If a knowledge graph is not built with **query efficiency in mind**, users will struggle to extract meaningful insights.

For instance, in a **medical knowledge graph**, if doctors frequently query: **"What are the symptoms of a given disease?"**,

the data model should allow **fast lookups** of disease-symptom relationships.

A well-structured schema for this query might look like:

```
MATCH (d:Disease {name: "Influenza"})-[:CAUSES]-
>(s:Symptom)
RETURN s.name
```

If symptoms were stored as **text properties instead of nodes**, querying them would be slow and inefficient.

A poor design choice:

```
CREATE (:Disease {name: "Influenza", symptoms:
"Fever, Cough, Sore Throat"})
```

This would require **string parsing** instead of simple relationship traversal, making it much harder to run AI-powered reasoning on symptoms.

5. Use Standardized Ontologies and Linked Data Principles

A knowledge graph becomes significantly more valuable when it **aligns with existing ontologies and data standards**. This allows it to **integrate with external knowledge sources**, making the graph more powerful and reusable.

For example, if building a knowledge graph for **scientific research**, instead of creating custom labels for diseases and drugs, align the graph with standards like **SNOMED CT (medical terminology) or DrugBank (pharmaceutical database)**.

Using Linked Data principles, external knowledge sources can be referenced via **URIs**:

```
@prefix dbo: <http://dbpedia.org/ontology/> .
@prefix dbr: <http://dbpedia.org/resource/> .
```

```
dbr:COVID-19 dbo:hasSymptom dbr:Fever .
```
By following this principle, the knowledge graph can **pull in external datasets and contribute to a broader linked data ecosystem**.

Common Mistakes and How to Avoid Them

1. Treating a Knowledge Graph Like a Relational Database

A common misconception is **forcing relational database structures into a graph model**. In relational databases, data is stored in tables with **primary keys and foreign keys**, whereas knowledge graphs store **relationships directly**.

Bad practice:

```
CREATE (:Person {name: "Bob", customer_id: "C123"})
CREATE (:CustomerInfo {customer_id: "C123",
address: "123 Main St"})
CREATE (:Transaction {transaction_id: "T001",
customer_id: "C123"})
```

This structure **mimics a relational database** and requires unnecessary joins to extract useful data.

Better approach:

```
CREATE (:Person {name: "Bob"})-[:LIVES_AT]-
>(:Address {street: "123 Main St"})
CREATE (:Person {name: "Bob"})-[:MADE]-
>(:Transaction {transaction_id: "T001"})
```

This allows direct traversal, avoiding unnecessary queries.

2. Storing Too Many Properties as Nodes Instead of Attributes

Not everything should be a node. If a property **does not represent a distinct entity**, it should be stored as an **attribute** rather than a separate node.

Bad practice:

```
CREATE (:Person {name: "Alice"})-[:HAS_AGE]->(:Age
{value: 30})
```
Better approach:

```
CREATE (:Person {name: "Alice", age: 30})
```
This **reduces unnecessary nodes**, improving query performance.

3. Ignoring Relationship Directions

Relationships should be modeled **with clear directionality** to avoid ambiguous queries.

Bad practice:

```
CREATE (:Person {name: "Alice"})-[:KNOWS]->(:Person
{name: "Bob"})
CREATE (:Person {name: "Bob"})-[:KNOWS]->(:Person
{name: "Alice"})
```

This creates redundant relationships. Instead, use a **single directional relationship** where it makes logical sense:

```
CREATE (:Person {name: "Alice"})-[:FRIENDS_WITH]-
>(:Person {name: "Bob"})
```

This ensures **consistent relationship traversal** without unnecessary duplications.

A well-designed knowledge graph **enables efficient querying, AI-driven reasoning, and seamless data integration**. Following best practices—such as defining clear relationships, optimizing for performance, and using standardized ontologies—ensures that the knowledge graph remains **scalable, maintainable, and useful**.

By avoiding common mistakes like **data redundancy, relational database thinking, and ambiguous relationships**, the knowledge graph can provide **meaningful, structured, and intelligent insights** that power AI-driven decision-making.

Chapter 5: Data Integration and Graph Construction

A knowledge graph is only as valuable as the data it contains. **No matter how well the graph is structured, if the data feeding into it is incomplete, inconsistent, or poorly linked, the graph will fail to deliver meaningful insights.**

Data integration and graph construction involve **gathering data from multiple sources, structuring it for graph representation, linking entities to ensure consistency, enriching the graph with additional insights, and maintaining data quality through cleaning and deduplication.**

This process requires a balance between **automation and manual oversight**. While AI-powered entity linking and automated Extract, Transform, Load (ETL) pipelines streamline the process, careful quality control ensures that errors do not compound over time.

Collecting and Structuring Data

Building a knowledge graph starts with **collecting the right data** and **structuring it properly**. The success of a knowledge graph depends on the **quality, consistency, and completeness** of its data. Without well-structured data, the graph will be fragmented, inefficient, and difficult to query, leading to unreliable results.

Data comes from various sources—databases, APIs, documents, logs, and even unstructured text. Each of these sources presents challenges in **integration, standardization, and representation**. The goal is to transform raw data into a **graph format where entities (nodes) and their relationships (edges) are clearly defined and linked**.

This process requires:

Identifying relevant data sources

Extracting and transforming data into a graph-friendly structure

Ensuring consistency in how entities and relationships are represented

Optimizing data models for efficient retrieval and reasoning

Let's break down these steps and explore practical methods for collecting and structuring data for a knowledge graph.

Identifying and Collecting Data Sources

Before structuring data, it's essential to determine **what data is needed** and **where it comes from**. The data sources depend on the purpose of the knowledge graph.

For example, if creating a **knowledge graph for financial fraud detection**, useful data sources might include:

Bank transaction logs (who is sending money to whom)

Customer databases (account holders, locations, risk profiles)

Publicly available fraud lists (sanctioned individuals, flagged companies)

Social connections (relationships between business partners and associates)

If building a **medical knowledge graph**, relevant sources could include:

Electronic Health Records (EHRs) (patient visits, diagnoses, treatments)

Clinical trial data (success rates of medications)

Medical ontologies (SNOMED CT, ICD codes)

Research papers (scientific publications about diseases and treatments)

These sources may exist in different formats: **structured (SQL, CSV, JSON), semi-structured (XML, logs, APIs), and unstructured (text, PDFs, web pages)**. The first challenge is extracting data and converting it into a usable structure.

Extracting and Structuring Data for Graph Representation

Once data is collected, it must be **transformed into a graph-friendly format** where entities and relationships are explicitly defined.

Step 1: Defining Core Entities and Relationships

A knowledge graph consists of **nodes (entities) and edges (relationships)**.

Nodes represent real-world objects like people, companies, diseases, or transactions.

Edges define how these entities are connected (e.g., "Alice OWNS Account A001", "COVID-19 CAUSES Fever").

For example, in a **fraud detection knowledge graph**, the core entities might be:

Customers (holding bank accounts)

Bank Accounts (used to send/receive transactions)

Transactions (money transfers between accounts)

The relationships define **how these entities interact**:

A Customer OWNS a Bank Account

A Transaction SENDS money FROM one Account TO another

A Transaction is FLAGGED as Suspicious

Step 2: Transforming Relational Data into Graph Format

Most raw data is stored in **relational databases**, where relationships are implicit in table joins. Before integrating this data into a knowledge graph, it must be **restructured into an explicit node-relationship format**.

For example, consider a **bank transaction database** with two tables:

Customer Table

Customer ID	Name	Email
C123	Alice	alice@email.com
C456	Bob	bob@email.com

Transaction Table

Transaction ID	Sender	Receiver	Amount	Date
T001	C123	C456	500	2023-08-01

Transaction ID	Sender	Receiver	Amount	Date
T002	C456	C123	200	2023-08-02

In a **graph format**, these tables become **nodes and relationships**:

```
CREATE (:Customer {id: "C123", name: "Alice",
email: "alice@email.com"})
CREATE (:Customer {id: "C456", name: "Bob", email:
"bob@email.com"})
CREATE (:Transaction {id: "T001", amount: 500,
date: "2023-08-01"})
CREATE (:Transaction {id: "T002", amount: 200,
date: "2023-08-02"})

MATCH (c1:Customer {id: "C123"}), (c2:Customer {id:
"C456"}), (t:Transaction {id: "T001"})
CREATE (c1)-[:SENDS]->(t)-[:TO]->(c2)

MATCH (c1:Customer {id: "C456"}), (c2:Customer {id:
"C123"}), (t:Transaction {id: "T002"})
CREATE (c1)-[:SENDS]->(t)-[:TO]->(c2)
```

Step 3: Structuring Semi-Structured and Unstructured Data

Not all data comes in clean tabular formats. **APIs, JSON files, XML, and text documents** need processing before they can be represented in a graph.

For example, a JSON API response for a **medical knowledge graph** might look like this:

```
{
  "disease": "Influenza",
  "symptoms": ["Fever", "Cough", "Fatigue"],
  "treatment": "Paracetamol"
}
```

To convert this into a graph structure:

```
CREATE (:Disease {name: "Influenza"})
CREATE (:Symptom {name: "Fever"})
CREATE (:Symptom {name: "Cough"})
CREATE (:Symptom {name: "Fatigue"})
```

```
CREATE (:Medication {name: "Paracetamol"})

MATCH (d:Disease {name: "Influenza"}), (s:Symptom
{name: "Fever"})
CREATE (d)-[:CAUSES]->(s)

MATCH (d:Disease {name: "Influenza"}),
(m:Medication {name: "Paracetamol"})
CREATE (m)-[:TREATS]->(d)
```

This approach **turns raw API data into a structured graph representation** that can be easily queried.

Ensuring Data Consistency and Integrity

Data collected from different sources often has **inconsistent formats**. Dates, currencies, names, and units must be standardized before integration.

For example, transactions may store dates in different formats:

"08/01/2023"

"2023-08-01"

"01-Aug-2023"

Before loading data into a graph, all dates should be converted to a **single format** to ensure consistency.

```
from datetime import datetime

# Convert inconsistent date formats to standard
YYYY-MM-DD
def standardize_date(date_str):
    return datetime.strptime(date_str,
"%m/%d/%Y").strftime("%Y-%m-%d")

print(standardize_date("08/01/2023"))  # Output:
"2023-08-01"
```

Validating Data Before Loading

It's essential to check for:

Missing values (a transaction without a sender or receiver is meaningless).

Duplicate entities (a customer appearing twice with different IDs).

Invalid relationships (a transaction pointing to a non-existent account).

A simple Cypher query to **detect transactions missing sender information**:

```
MATCH (t:Transaction) WHERE NOT (t)-[:SENDS]->()
RETURN t
```

This ensures **only complete, valid data enters the graph**.

Collecting and structuring data for a knowledge graph requires careful planning to ensure **data quality, consistency, and efficiency**. By identifying **relevant data sources, transforming relational data into a graph format, linking entities correctly, and standardizing formats**, the knowledge graph becomes a **robust foundation for AI-driven insights**.

A well-structured knowledge graph allows AI to **discover patterns, infer new knowledge, and provide meaningful answers**—turning raw data into actionable intelligence.

Entity Linking and Data Enrichment

A knowledge graph is only useful if it accurately represents **real-world entities and their relationships**. However, raw data often comes from multiple sources, each using different names, formats, and identifiers for the same entities. **Entity linking ensures that different references to the same entity are recognized as one unified entity**, preventing fragmentation and redundancy in the knowledge graph.

Once entities are correctly linked, **data enrichment enhances these entities by integrating additional context, attributes, and relationships**, making the knowledge graph more informative and valuable. Together, **entity linking and data enrichment create a structured, intelligent knowledge graph** that can power AI-driven decision-making, semantic search, fraud detection, recommendation systems, and more.

Entity Linking: Identifying and Merging Equivalent Entities

Entity linking is the process of **matching different records that refer to the same entity**, even when they are named differently across datasets. This step is critical in preventing duplicate nodes and ensuring **relationships between entities are not fragmented**.

Why Entity Linking is Necessary

When multiple data sources are combined, entities may appear under:

Different names ("John Doe" vs. "J. Doe" vs. "Jonathan Doe")

Different formats ("Company X Ltd." vs. "Company X Limited")

Different identifiers (customer ID in one database, tax ID in another)

If these discrepancies are not resolved, the knowledge graph becomes cluttered with duplicate nodes, leading to misleading query results.

For example, in a **financial fraud detection knowledge graph**, an entity appearing twice under slightly different names could result in an incomplete fraud analysis. If a fraudster has **multiple bank accounts under variations of their name**, failing to link these entities means the AI might miss critical connections in transaction patterns.

Techniques for Entity Linking

Entity linking relies on **exact matching, probabilistic similarity, and machine learning models** to unify records.

1. Exact Matching Using Unique Identifiers

If an entity has a unique ID, it can be used to merge records automatically.

For example, in a **customer database**, entity linking can be done using **email addresses** or **government-issued IDs**.

```
MERGE (c:Customer {email: "alice@email.com"})
ON CREATE SET c.name = "Alice", c.customer_id =
"C123"
```

This ensures that if "Alice" already exists in the graph, a duplicate **is not created**.

2. Probabilistic Matching for Name Variations

When unique IDs are not available, **similarity algorithms** can identify potential matches based on name, address, or other attributes.

For example, if merging customer records:

Name	Email	Address
John Doe	john@email.com	123 Elm St, NY
J. Doe	jdoe@email.com	123 Elm Street, NYC
Jonathan D	j.doe@email.com	123 Elm St, New York

A **Levenshtein distance algorithm** can compare name similarity, while **Jaccard similarity** can compare addresses.

A simple Python example for comparing entity names:

```
from fuzzywuzzy import fuzz

name1 = "John Doe"
name2 = "J. Doe"

similarity_score = fuzz.ratio(name1, name2)
print("Similarity Score:", similarity_score)
```

If the similarity score is above a threshold (e.g., 90%), the entities can be considered **a match** and merged in the knowledge graph.

3. AI-Based Entity Resolution

Machine learning models trained on large datasets can **automatically learn patterns in entity duplication**. These models use:

Neural networks for learning entity representation.

Graph embeddings to identify duplicate nodes based on their relationships.

For example, Neo4j's **Graph Data Science Library** can detect duplicate entities using **Node Similarity algorithms**.

A simple **Cypher query** to find similar entities:

```
CALL gds.nodeSimilarity.stream({
  nodeProjection: 'Customer',
  relationshipProjection: 'OWNS',
  similarityCutoff: 0.85
})
YIELD node1, node2, similarity
RETURN gds.util.asNode(node1).name,
gds.util.asNode(node2).name, similarity
```

This **compares customer nodes based on their relationships** (e.g., shared addresses or accounts) and **identifies potential duplicates**.

Data Enrichment: Adding Context and Intelligence to Entities

Once entities are correctly linked, **data enrichment** adds additional context, attributes, and relationships to improve the quality and usefulness of the knowledge graph.

Why Data Enrichment Matters

An entity without rich information is **less useful**. A knowledge graph enriched with additional data allows AI to:

Make better recommendations (e.g., personalized product suggestions in an e-commerce knowledge graph).

Detect anomalies more accurately (e.g., flagging suspicious transactions by analyzing customer spending patterns).

Provide deeper insights (e.g., linking diseases to scientific research papers in a medical knowledge graph).

Examples of Data Enrichment

1. Enriching a Financial Knowledge Graph with External Data

If a knowledge graph tracks **companies and their transactions**, additional data can be integrated to improve fraud detection.

Before enrichment:

Company A owns 3 bank accounts.

These accounts send large wire transfers.

85

After enrichment:

Company A is flagged on a government **sanctions list**.

Its CEO was previously **convicted of money laundering**.

Transactions correlate with **offshore accounts known for fraud**.

This enriched data allows AI to **detect fraud risks** that would otherwise go unnoticed.

A **Cypher query** to integrate **sanctions list data** into a financial knowledge graph:

```
MATCH (c:Company {name: "Company A"}),
(s:SanctionsList {entity: "Company A"})
MERGE (c)-[:FLAGGED_ON]->(s)
```

Now, if AI queries companies flagged on a sanctions list, it can **quickly identify high-risk entities**.

2. Enriching a Medical Knowledge Graph with Scientific Research

A medical knowledge graph tracking **diseases and treatments** can be enriched with **clinical trial data**.

If a node represents **COVID-19**, enrichment might include:

Latest research papers on COVID-19 treatments

Clinical trials for antiviral drugs

Hospital records on COVID-19 patient recovery rates

A **Cypher query to enrich a disease entity with research papers**:

```
MATCH (d:Disease {name: "COVID-19"}),
(r:ResearchPaper {title: "Effectiveness of
Remdesivir"})
CREATE (d)-[:HAS_RESEARCH]->(r)
```

Now, querying **related research on COVID-19** becomes instant, enabling **AI-powered medical recommendations**.

Integrating Entity Linking and Data Enrichment in ETL Pipelines

For large-scale knowledge graphs, entity linking and data enrichment should be automated using **ETL (Extract, Transform, Load) pipelines**.

A Python **ETL pipeline** for linking and enriching customer entities using Neo4j:

```python
from neo4j import GraphDatabase

# Connect to Neo4j
uri = "bolt://localhost:7687"
driver = GraphDatabase.driver(uri, auth=("neo4j",
"password"))

def link_customers(tx):
    query = """
    MATCH (c1:Customer), (c2:Customer)
    WHERE c1.email = c2.email AND id(c1) < id(c2)
    MERGE (c1)-[:SAME_AS]->(c2)
    """
    tx.run(query)

def enrich_customers(tx):
    query = """
    MATCH (c:Customer), (r:RiskScore {customer_id:
c.id})
    MERGE (c)-[:HAS_RISK_SCORE]->(r)
    """
    tx.run(query)

# Execute the entity linking and enrichment
with driver.session() as session:
    session.write_transaction(link_customers)
    session.write_transaction(enrich_customers)

print("Entity linking and enrichment completed!")
```

This pipeline:

Links duplicate customers based on email.

Enriches customers with external risk scores.

Entity linking ensures that **all references to the same real-world entity are unified**, eliminating duplicates and inconsistencies. Data enrichment **adds depth and intelligence**, making the knowledge graph more useful for AI applications.

By implementing **automated entity resolution, similarity detection, and data enrichment techniques**, knowledge graphs become **highly structured, deeply connected, and insightful**, enabling **advanced analytics, AI-powered recommendations, and fraud detection**.

Cleaning, Deduplication, and Graph ETL Pipelines

Data is rarely perfect when it arrives for integration into a knowledge graph. It often contains **inconsistencies, missing values, duplicate records, and formatting issues**. If these issues are not addressed, they can lead to **incorrect relationships, unreliable insights, and performance bottlenecks**.

To ensure a **high-quality, structured, and optimized** knowledge graph, raw data must go through **cleaning, deduplication, and transformation** before being loaded into the graph database. This is where **ETL (Extract, Transform, Load) pipelines** come into play—automating the process of **collecting, cleaning, structuring, and loading data** into the knowledge graph.

Cleaning: Standardizing and Fixing Data Issues

Before data is loaded into a knowledge graph, it must be **validated and standardized** to ensure **consistency, accuracy, and completeness**.

Handling Inconsistent Data Formats

Raw data often arrives in different formats. Dates, addresses, phone numbers, and currencies may be recorded inconsistently. If left unprocessed, this inconsistency will cause errors when querying the graph.

For example, a **customer database** might store birthdates in multiple formats:

`08/01/1990`

1990-08-01

1st August 1990

To standardize dates before inserting them into the graph, a Python script can **convert all date formats into ISO-8601 format** (YYYY-MM-DD):

```
from datetime import datetime

def standardize_date(date_str):
    formats = ["%m/%d/%Y", "%Y-%m-%d", "%d %B %Y"]
    for fmt in formats:
        try:
            return datetime.strptime(date_str,
fmt).strftime("%Y-%m-%d")
        except ValueError:
            continue
    return None   # Return None for unprocessable
dates

print(standardize_date("08/01/1990"))   # Output:
"1990-08-01"
print(standardize_date("1st August 1990"))   #
Output: "1990-08-01"
```

Before inserting a date into the knowledge graph, we should **convert all values into this standardized format**.

Detecting and Filling Missing Data

Missing values weaken the knowledge graph. If a **customer node lacks an email address**, certain relationships (such as linking accounts across datasets) may fail.

A simple **Cypher query to identify missing attributes** in Neo4j:

```
MATCH (c:Customer) WHERE c.email IS NULL RETURN c.name, c.id
```

If data is missing, it can be **filled using enrichment techniques,** such as:

Using external datasets (e.g., fetching company metadata from an open database).

Interpolating missing values (e.g., estimating missing sensor readings).

89

Flagging incomplete nodes for manual review.

For example, if customer phone numbers are missing, we can integrate data from an external contact database:

```
MATCH (c:Customer), (p:PhoneRecord)
WHERE c.name = p.name AND c.phone IS NULL
SET c.phone = p.phone
```

Deduplication: Merging Duplicate Entities

A knowledge graph should **represent each entity uniquely**. However, duplicate entities often arise when data is sourced from **multiple datasets**, where the same entity may appear with different formats or slightly different spellings.

For example, a **person** may be listed multiple times:

"John Doe"

"J. Doe"

"Jonathan Doe"

Without deduplication, a knowledge graph will create separate nodes for each variation, **fragmenting relationships and weakening insights**.

Detecting Duplicate Entities

To find possible duplicates in Neo4j, we can use **similarity algorithms**:

```
CALL gds.nodeSimilarity.stream({
  nodeProjection: 'Person',
  relationshipProjection: 'KNOWS',
  similarityCutoff: 0.85
})
YIELD node1, node2, similarity
RETURN gds.util.asNode(node1).name,
gds.util.asNode(node2).name, similarity
```

This query finds **similar entities** based on shared connections. If two customer nodes **own the same accounts** and **share the same phone number**, they are likely duplicates.

Merging Duplicate Entities

Once duplicates are detected, they must be merged. In Neo4j, the **MERGE** statement ensures that **only one node exists for each unique entity**:

```
MATCH (p1:Person), (p2:Person)
WHERE p1.name = p2.name AND id(p1) < id(p2)
MERGE (p1)-[:SAME_AS]->(p2)
```

After linking duplicate nodes, a script can **merge their properties and relationships**:

```
MATCH (p1:Person)-[:SAME_AS]->(p2:Person)
SET p1.email = coalesce(p1.email, p2.email),
    p1.phone = coalesce(p1.phone, p2.phone)
DETACH DELETE p2
```

Now, "John Doe" and "J. Doe" are merged into **one single entity** with a unified set of relationships.

Graph ETL Pipelines: Automating Data Integration

Knowledge graphs often require continuous updates from multiple sources. **ETL pipelines automate the process of extracting, transforming, and loading data into the graph**, ensuring that it remains up-to-date and structured.

A typical **Graph ETL pipeline** consists of:

Extracting data from databases, APIs, or files.

Cleaning and transforming data (standardization, deduplication, enrichment).

Loading data into the knowledge graph for efficient querying.

Step 1: Extract Data from External Sources

For example, an **ETL pipeline for financial transactions** may extract data from a SQL database:

```
import pandas as pd
import psycopg2

# Connect to SQL database
```

```
conn = psycopg2.connect("dbname=bank user=postgres
password=securepassword")
query = "SELECT customer_id, name, email, balance
FROM customers"
df = pd.read_sql(query, conn)

print(df.head())   # Display extracted data
```

Step 2: Transform Data (Cleaning & Deduplication)

Before inserting data into the knowledge graph, we clean missing values and detect duplicates:

```
# Standardize email case
df['email'] = df['email'].str.lower()

# Fill missing phone numbers from another source
phone_data = pd.read_csv("phone_numbers.csv")
df = df.merge(phone_data, on="customer_id",
how="left")
```

Step 3: Load Data into the Graph

Once cleaned, the data is **ingested into Neo4j**:

```
from neo4j import GraphDatabase

driver =
GraphDatabase.driver("bolt://localhost:7687",
auth=("neo4j", "password"))

def insert_customer(tx, id, name, email, balance):
    tx.run("""
    MERGE (c:Customer {id: $id})
    ON CREATE SET c.name = $name, c.email = $email,
c.balance = $balance
    """, id=id, name=name, email=email,
balance=balance)

with driver.session() as session:
    for _, row in df.iterrows():
        session.write_transaction(insert_customer,
row['customer_id'], row['name'], row['email'],
row['balance'])
```

```
print("Data successfully loaded into Neo4j!")
```

This ETL pipeline ensures that **new customer records are added, duplicate records are merged, and attributes are updated automatically**.

A well-structured knowledge graph requires **clean, deduplicated, and structured data**.

Cleaning ensures data is standardized and free of errors.

Deduplication merges duplicate entities, preventing fragmentation.

Graph ETL pipelines automate the process of extracting, transforming, and loading data.

By implementing **automated data validation, entity resolution, and continuous ETL processing**, knowledge graphs remain **accurate, scalable, and insightful**, powering **AI-driven analytics, fraud detection, and intelligent search systems**.

Chapter 6: Graph Databases and Query Languages

Knowledge graphs are most effective when stored in **graph databases**, which are designed to handle **complex relationships and interconnected data**. Unlike relational databases that rely on tables and joins, graph databases allow data to be **represented as nodes (entities) and edges (relationships)**, enabling **efficient queries and deep insights**.

To effectively interact with knowledge graphs, specialized **query languages** such as **SPARQL, Cypher, and Gremlin** are used. These languages provide the ability to **retrieve, analyze, and manipulate graph data** in a way that traditional SQL cannot.

Selecting the right graph database depends on **performance, scalability, data model compatibility, and integration needs**. This chapter explores the leading graph databases, their query languages, and how to choose the best fit for your specific use case.

Overview of Popular Graph Databases

Graph databases have revolutionized the way **complex relationships and connected data** are stored and queried. Unlike traditional relational databases, which rely on **tables and joins**, graph databases represent data as **nodes (entities) and edges (relationships)**. This structure allows queries to be **faster, more intuitive, and better suited for applications that rely on highly connected data**.

Choosing the right graph database depends on **data structure, scalability, query language support, and integration with other systems**. While **Neo4j, Amazon Neptune, and ArangoDB** are among the most widely used, there are several other options, each designed to handle different workloads and use cases.

Neo4j: The Leading Graph Database for Relationship-Driven Applications

Neo4j is one of the most widely used **property graph databases**, designed for **highly connected data**. It follows a **native graph storage model**, which means **nodes and relationships are stored directly, rather than being simulated using relational joins**. This makes it ideal for applications that **require deep traversal queries**, such as **fraud detection, recommendation engines, and knowledge graphs**.

Core Features of Neo4j

Property Graph Model: Data is stored as **nodes, relationships, and properties**, allowing for **rich, structured representation**.

Cypher Query Language: Neo4j uses **Cypher**, a query language designed specifically for graph traversal, which is both **intuitive and expressive**.

Highly Optimized for Deep Relationships: Queries that would be expensive in a relational database—such as **finding all people within three degrees of connection**—are extremely fast in Neo4j.

Graph Data Science (GDS) Library: Provides advanced **graph algorithms** for **centrality, community detection, and pathfinding**.

Scalability: Supports **high availability clustering and sharding**, making it suitable for large-scale enterprise applications.

Example Use Case: Fraud Detection in Banking

Financial institutions use Neo4j to **identify fraudulent transactions** by analyzing the relationships between customers, accounts, and transactions. A common fraud pattern involves **money being moved in circles across multiple accounts to obscure its origin**.

Graph Representation of Transactions in Neo4j

```
CREATE (:Customer {name: "Alice", id: "C123"})
CREATE (:Customer {name: "Bob", id: "C456"})
CREATE (:Account {account_number: "A001"})
CREATE (:Account {account_number: "A002"})
CREATE (:Transaction {id: "T001", amount: 500,
date: "2023-08-01"})

MATCH (c1:Customer {id: "C123"}), (a1:Account
{account_number: "A001"})
CREATE (c1)-[:OWNS]->(a1)
```

```
MATCH (c2:Customer {id: "C456"}), (a2:Account
{account_number: "A002"})
CREATE (c2)-[:OWNS]->(a2)

MATCH (a1:Account {account_number: "A001"}),
(a2:Account {account_number: "A002"}),
(t:Transaction {id: "T001"})
CREATE (a1)-[:SENDS {amount: t.amount, date:
t.date}]->(a2)
```

This structure allows for **fraud detection algorithms** to identify suspicious circular money transfers.

Who Should Use Neo4j?

Neo4j is best suited for organizations that:

Need **deep relationship queries** (e.g., fraud detection, social networks).

Want a **fast and expressive graph query language** (Cypher).

Require **real-time graph analytics and machine learning integration**.

Amazon Neptune: A Cloud-Native Graph Database for Large-Scale Applications

Amazon Neptune is a **fully managed graph database service** designed for **cloud-based, large-scale applications**. Unlike Neo4j, which focuses on **property graphs**, Neptune supports **both RDF (for semantic graphs) and property graphs (for highly connected data)**.

Core Features of Amazon Neptune

Supports Multiple Query Languages: It is compatible with **SPARQL (for RDF graphs)** and Gremlin (for property graphs).

Fully Managed and Serverless: Scales automatically, reducing the need for manual infrastructure management.

Seamless Integration with AWS Ecosystem: Works well with **Lambda, SageMaker (AI), and S3 storage**.

Graph Data Processing at Scale: Optimized for **real-time query performance on massive datasets**.

Example Use Case: Knowledge Graph for Medical Research

Amazon Neptune is often used to build **knowledge graphs for healthcare**, linking diseases, treatments, clinical trials, and medical research papers.

SPARQL Query to Retrieve Treatments for a Disease

```
PREFIX dbo: <http://dbpedia.org/ontology/>
SELECT ?treatment WHERE {
  ?disease dbo:name "Influenza" .
  ?disease dbo:treatment ?treatment .
}
```

This query **fetches all known treatments** for **Influenza** in a structured knowledge graph.

Who Should Use Amazon Neptune?

Amazon Neptune is ideal for organizations that:

Need **cloud-native scalability** and **managed services**.

Require **support for both property graphs (Gremlin) and RDF (SPARQL)**.

Are working with **semantic web, linked data, or massive-scale graph queries**.

ArangoDB: A Multi-Model Graph Database for Hybrid Workloads

ArangoDB is a **multi-model database**, meaning it supports **graph, document, and key-value storage in a single system**. This makes it a great choice when a project requires **both document storage and graph traversal capabilities**.

Core Features of ArangoDB

Graph + Document Storage: Supports **AQL (ArangoDB Query Language)**, allowing **SQL-like graph queries**.

Flexible Schema: Allows storing **documents (JSON-like data) alongside graphs**.

Sharding & Replication: Designed for **high availability and distributed clusters**.

Integrated Graph Analytics: Includes **graph traversal algorithms** for shortest path, community detection, and more.

Example Use Case: Product Recommendation System

A **recommendation engine** can use ArangoDB to suggest products based on **user behavior and social connections**.

AQL Query to Find Related Products

```
FOR v, e IN 1..2 OUTBOUND "products/SmartphoneX"
GRAPH "ProductGraph"
RETURN v.name
```

This query **retrieves products that are linked** to **SmartphoneX** within **two degrees of connection** (e.g., accessories, similar models).

Who Should Use ArangoDB?

ArangoDB is a good choice for:

Applications requiring **both document and graph storage**.

Large-scale **distributed graph workloads**.

Developers who prefer **a flexible, multi-model database approach**.

Each graph database serves different needs:

Neo4j is best for **real-time graph analytics, relationship-heavy queries, and fraud detection**.

Amazon Neptune is great for **cloud-based applications needing RDF/SPARQL or property graphs**.

ArangoDB is ideal for **hybrid document-graph storage with flexible data modeling**.

When choosing a graph database, consider **query language, scalability, cloud integration, and analytical capabilities**. The right database will enable **faster queries, deeper insights, and better AI-powered decision-making**.

Querying Knowledge Graphs

Knowledge graphs are only as useful as the ability to **retrieve and analyze** the information they contain. Unlike traditional databases that rely on **SQL for tabular data**, knowledge graphs require specialized **graph query languages** that are designed to handle **nodes, relationships, and complex patterns** efficiently.

There are three major query languages used in graph databases:

SPARQL, which is used for **RDF (Resource Description Framework) graphs** and is particularly useful for **semantic knowledge graphs, linked data, and ontologies**.

Cypher, which is optimized for **property graphs**, such as those used in **Neo4j**, and provides an intuitive **pattern-based syntax** for querying relationships.

Gremlin, a **graph traversal language** used in **multi-model and distributed graph databases**, such as **JanusGraph, Amazon Neptune, and Azure Cosmos DB**.

Each of these languages serves a different **data model and querying style**, making them more suitable for different types of applications. Understanding **how they work and when to use them** is crucial to designing **efficient, scalable, and intelligent** knowledge graph solutions.

SPARQL: Querying RDF-Based Knowledge Graphs

SPARQL (**SPARQL Protocol and RDF Query Language**) is the standard query language for **RDF (Resource Description Framework) knowledge graphs**. RDF is widely used in **semantic web applications, ontologies, and linked data**.

How SPARQL Works

SPARQL queries use a **triple pattern matching approach**, where data is stored as **subject-predicate-object triples**. Each triple represents a **fact** in the knowledge graph.

For example, in a **medical knowledge graph**, the following RDF triples might exist:

```
:Disease1   rdf:type   :Disease .
:Disease1   :name   "Influenza" .
:Disease1   :causes   :Symptom1 .
:Symptom1   :name   "Fever" .
```

These triples describe **Influenza as a disease that causes Fever**.

SPARQL Query to Find Symptoms of Influenza

To retrieve all symptoms linked to **Influenza**, a SPARQL query would look like this:

```
PREFIX dbo: <http://dbpedia.org/ontology/>

SELECT ?symptom WHERE {
  ?disease dbo:name "Influenza" .
  ?disease dbo:causes ?symptom .
}
```

This query searches the knowledge graph for **any entity that has a "causes" relationship with "Influenza"**, returning all symptoms.

When to Use SPARQL?

SPARQL is best suited for **semantic web applications, knowledge graphs, and datasets that rely on linked open data**. It is commonly used in:

Healthcare and biomedical knowledge graphs (e.g., linking diseases to treatments).

Government and open data projects (e.g., querying public datasets like Wikidata).

Enterprise knowledge graphs (e.g., integrating company data across different systems).

Cypher: Querying Property Graphs in Neo4j

Cypher is a **pattern-based query language** designed specifically for **property graphs**, where data is structured as **nodes, relationships, and properties**. It is used in **Neo4j and other property graph databases**.

How Cypher Works

Cypher uses **ASCII-art-like syntax** that visually represents graph patterns, making it **intuitive and expressive**.

For example, in a **social network knowledge graph**, we might have:

```
(:Person {name: "Alice"})-[:FRIENDS_WITH]->(:Person
{name: "Bob"})
```
This structure means **Alice is friends with Bob**.

Cypher Query to Find All Friends of Alice

```
MATCH (p:Person)-[:FRIENDS_WITH]->(friend)
WHERE p.name = "Alice"
RETURN friend.name
```

This query **finds all people connected to Alice** through the **FRIENDS_WITH** relationship.

Cypher Query to Find Friends of Friends (Second-Degree Connections)

```
MATCH (p:Person)-[:FRIENDS_WITH]->()-
[:FRIENDS_WITH]->(friend)
WHERE p.name = "Alice"
RETURN friend.name
```

This retrieves **people who are connected to Alice's friends**, allowing for **network analysis, recommendation systems, and influencer detection**.

Using Cypher for Fraud Detection

In a **financial fraud detection system**, we can track **suspicious money transfers** by detecting circular transactions:

```
MATCH (a1:Account)-[:SENDS]->(t1:Transaction)-
[:TO]->(a2:Account),
       (a2)-[:SENDS]->(t2:Transaction)-[:TO]-
>(a3:Account),
       (a3)-[:SENDS]->(t3:Transaction)-[:TO]->(a1)
RETURN a1, a2, a3
```

This query finds cases where **money is transferred in a loop**, a common pattern in **money laundering schemes**.

When to Use Cypher?

Cypher is best suited for **graph databases where relationships are central to the analysis**, including:

Fraud detection in financial networks (tracking money flows).

Social networks and recommendation systems (finding connections between users).

Enterprise knowledge graphs (representing company structures and dependencies).

Gremlin: A Graph Traversal Language for Distributed Graphs

Gremlin is a **graph traversal language** that is used in **multi-model and distributed graph databases**, such as **JanusGraph, Amazon Neptune, and Azure Cosmos DB**. Unlike Cypher, which is declarative, Gremlin is **procedural**, meaning queries describe **how to traverse the graph step by step**.

How Gremlin Works

Gremlin represents queries as **chained traversal steps**.

For example, in a **knowledge graph of employees and companies**, the structure might be:

```
g.V().has("name",
"Alice").out("WORKS_FOR").values("company")
```
This query **retrieves the company where Alice works**.

Gremlin Query to Find Mutual Friends

```
g.V().has("name",
"Alice").out("FRIENDS_WITH").out("FRIENDS_WITH").de
dup().values("name")
```

This retrieves **all people who are connected to Alice's friends**, similar to Cypher's second-degree connections query.

Gremlin Query for Pathfinding (Shortest Route Between Two Entities)

```
g.V().has("name",
"Alice").repeat(out().simplePath()).until(has("name
", "Bob")).path()
```

This query **finds the shortest path between Alice and Bob**, useful for **supply chain management, logistics, and recommendation engines**.

When to Use Gremlin?

Gremlin is well-suited for **large-scale, distributed graph processing**, including:

Cloud-based knowledge graphs (Amazon Neptune, JanusGraph).

IoT and network analysis (tracking device connections).

Complex pathfinding and traversal-heavy queries.

Comparing SPARQL, Cypher, and Gremlin

Feature	SPARQL	Cypher	Gremlin
Graph Type	RDF (Semantic)	Property Graph	Property Graph
Best for	Ontologies, Linked Data	Social networks, Fraud detection	Distributed graphs, IoT, Pathfinding
Query Style	Declarative (Triple-based)	Declarative (Pattern-based)	Procedural (Step-based)

Feature	SPARQL	Cypher	Gremlin
Common Use Cases	Healthcare, Open Data	Social Networks, Fraud Detection	Network Analysis, Supply Chains
Example Database	Amazon Neptune, Virtuoso	Neo4j, ArangoDB	JanusGraph, CosmosDB

SPARQL, Cypher, and Gremlin each serve different **types of knowledge graphs**:

SPARQL is best for semantic web, RDF data, and ontologies.

Cypher excels in property graph databases like Neo4j for relationship-heavy queries.

Gremlin is ideal for traversal-based queries in large, distributed graph systems.

Understanding the strengths of each query language ensures that **knowledge graphs can be queried efficiently and effectively**, enabling AI, analytics, and intelligent decision-making.

Choosing the Right Graph Database

Selecting the right graph database is one of the most important decisions when building a **knowledge graph, recommendation engine, fraud detection system, or any application requiring complex relationship queries**. A graph database is **not just about storing data**—it needs to be **fast, scalable, and optimized for the type of queries your application will run**.

Many factors influence this choice, including **data model compatibility, query language support, scalability, cloud integration, and real-time performance**. Different graph databases excel in different areas, and choosing the wrong one can lead to performance bottlenecks, high infrastructure costs, or even the inability to efficiently retrieve data.

To make an informed decision, it's essential to understand **how your data is structured, what queries will be executed, and what level of scalability and maintenance effort is required**.

Before deciding on a graph database, the first step is to analyze **how data will be stored, connected, and queried**. The structure of the graph and the expected query patterns determine **which database will perform best for your use case**.

A financial fraud detection system, for instance, requires **complex pattern-matching across multiple accounts and transactions**. A **knowledge graph for scientific research** may need **semantic reasoning and RDF support**. A **social media application** will focus on **deep relationship traversals, such as friend recommendations and influence scoring**.

Defining the Graph Model

There are two main graph models used in graph databases:

Property Graphs, which store data as **nodes (entities), relationships (edges), and properties (attributes on nodes and edges)**. These graphs are used in **Neo4j, Amazon Neptune, ArangoDB, and JanusGraph**.

RDF Graphs, which store data as **subject-predicate-object triples**. These are typically used in **semantic web applications, ontologies, and linked data projects** and are supported by **Amazon Neptune, Virtuoso, and GraphDB**.

Choosing between these models depends on **whether the application needs semantic reasoning and linked data (RDF) or highly connected property graphs with flexible attributes**.

Evaluating Graph Databases Based on Performance and Scalability

Once the graph model is clear, the next step is evaluating **performance, scalability, and ease of use**.

Neo4j, for example, is optimized for **fast traversals and complex relationship queries**, making it an excellent choice for **fraud detection, recommendation systems, and social networks**.

Amazon Neptune provides **cloud-native scalability and supports both property and RDF graphs**, making it a great option for **large-scale knowledge graphs and semantic web applications**.

ArangoDB offers a **multi-model approach**, meaning it supports **both document and graph storage**, making it useful when data needs to be queried in multiple ways.

The scalability factor is particularly important for applications that will handle **millions or billions of nodes and relationships**. Distributed graph databases like **JanusGraph** and **TigerGraph** are designed for handling **big data workloads and real-time analytics** across multiple servers.

Comparing Query Languages and Developer Experience

Different graph databases use different query languages, and the choice of language affects **developer productivity, query complexity, and learning curve**.

Neo4j uses **Cypher**, which is an intuitive, **pattern-based query language** that makes it easy to **express complex relationship queries**. A simple Cypher query to find friends of a user looks like this:

```
MATCH (p:Person)-[:FRIENDS_WITH]->(friend)
WHERE p.name = "Alice"
RETURN friend.name
```

SPARQL, used in **RDF-based graph databases**, is optimized for **semantic reasoning and linked data queries**. A SPARQL query to fetch books written by J.K. Rowling looks like this:

```
PREFIX dbo: <http://dbpedia.org/ontology/>
SELECT ?book WHERE {
   ?book dbo:author
<http://dbpedia.org/resource/J.K._Rowling> .
}
```

Gremlin, used in **multi-model and distributed graph databases**, is a **graph traversal language** that allows for step-by-step graph navigation. Finding mutual friends using Gremlin looks like this:

```
g.V().has("name",
"Alice").out("FRIENDS_WITH").out("FRIENDS_WITH").de
dup().values("name")
```

For developers who prefer **an easy-to-learn, SQL-like syntax, Cypher** is often the best choice. For **semantic applications requiring reasoning and ontologies, SPARQL** is essential. For **large-scale distributed graphs with complex traversals, Gremlin** is a strong candidate.

Real-World Use Cases and Database Selection

A **financial crime detection system** that tracks money laundering across multiple accounts needs a database capable of **deep graph traversal, fraud pattern detection, and high-speed queries**. Neo4j is a strong choice for this scenario because of its **efficient pathfinding algorithms and graph analytics capabilities**.

An **e-commerce recommendation engine** that suggests products based on customer behavior and product similarities benefits from **fast neighbor-based queries**. ArangoDB is a suitable choice, as it **combines graph relationships with document storage** for tracking product attributes and user preferences in one system.

A **global knowledge graph for medical research** needs **linked open data, ontologies, and semantic reasoning**. Amazon Neptune or Virtuoso, both supporting **RDF and SPARQL**, are well-suited for this application, as they allow **integration with external knowledge sources like Wikidata and PubMed**.

A **telecom network analytics system** that analyzes **network failures, device connectivity, and anomaly detection** benefits from a **highly scalable, distributed graph database**. JanusGraph, which runs on **Apache Cassandra or HBase**, is a great fit for handling **billions of edges across distributed clusters**.

Final Considerations: Deployment, Cost, and Maintenance

Beyond performance and query capabilities, practical considerations such as **deployment model, cost, and maintenance effort** also influence database selection.

For a **fully managed cloud solution**, Amazon Neptune eliminates the need for database maintenance and **automatically scales with demand**.

For organizations needing **on-premise control and fine-tuned performance**, Neo4j's **self-hosted enterprise version** allows for greater customization and data security.

For startups and developers looking for **an open-source, multi-model approach**, ArangoDB provides **graph + document database functionality with community support**.

For applications that require **extreme scalability and real-time analytics**, distributed graph databases like **TigerGraph and JanusGraph** are designed to **scale horizontally across large datasets**.

Selecting the right graph database is about **understanding data structure, query patterns, scalability needs, and deployment constraints**.

A **property graph database** like **Neo4j** is best for **relationship-heavy applications** such as **fraud detection, social networks, and recommendation engines**.

An **RDF-based graph database** like **Amazon Neptune or Virtuoso** is ideal for **semantic reasoning, linked data, and knowledge graphs**.

A **distributed graph database** like **JanusGraph or TigerGraph** is required for **big data workloads, telecom networks, and large-scale analytics**.

A **multi-model graph database** like **ArangoDB** is useful when **combining document and graph storage in hybrid applications**.

The best choice depends on **the complexity of relationships, expected query volume, and whether the system requires semantic reasoning, real-time analytics, or deep graph traversals**. By aligning the database with the specific needs of the application, organizations can ensure **efficient performance, long-term scalability, and insightful data exploration**.

Chapter 7: Knowledge Graphs for Machine Learning

Machine learning thrives on **structured, high-quality data**. Traditional datasets—tables of numerical values, categorical features, and text—are useful but often fail to **capture real-world relationships and context** effectively. Knowledge graphs bridge this gap by providing **rich, interconnected representations** of data, enabling AI models to learn in a way that **mimics human reasoning**.

By integrating knowledge graphs into machine learning pipelines, AI models gain access to **contextual knowledge, hidden relationships, and logical inferences**, leading to **more accurate predictions, better explainability, and reduced data sparsity**.

How Knowledge Graphs Improve AI Models

Artificial intelligence models are only as good as the data they learn from. Traditional machine learning relies on structured datasets—rows and columns that capture attributes but fail to represent **the connections and relationships between different data points**. This lack of structure limits the ability of AI models to reason, infer, and make context-aware decisions.

A **knowledge graph** provides **contextual intelligence** by structuring data as **nodes (entities) and edges (relationships)**, preserving the **meaningful connections** that exist in real-world scenarios. When integrated into AI models, knowledge graphs enable **better generalization, improved explainability, and enhanced learning from limited data**.

Traditional AI models struggle when dealing with **high-dimensional, sparse, or disconnected data**. A knowledge graph provides a **structured way to store and retrieve information**, allowing models to learn from **both explicit facts and inferred knowledge**.

For example, in a **medical diagnosis system**, a deep learning model trained on raw patient data might predict that a person has **flu-like symptoms**, but without a structured way to **link symptoms to diseases**, it may struggle to differentiate between **influenza, COVID-19, or pneumonia**. A knowledge graph **links symptoms, diseases, treatments, and risk factors**, helping the AI model make **better-informed predictions**.

Example: Representing Medical Knowledge in a Graph Database

In a Neo4j knowledge graph, the relationships between diseases, symptoms, and treatments can be structured like this:

```
CREATE (:Disease {name: "Influenza"})
CREATE (:Symptom {name: "Fever"})
CREATE (:Symptom {name: "Cough"})
CREATE (:Treatment {name: "Paracetamol"})

MATCH (d:Disease {name: "Influenza"}), (s:Symptom
{name: "Fever"})
CREATE (d)-[:CAUSES]->(s)

MATCH (d:Disease {name: "Influenza"}), (t:Treatment
{name: "Paracetamol"})
CREATE (t)-[:TREATS]->(d)
```

Now, an AI model predicting **Influenza** can use this **graph structure** to not only detect symptoms but also **suggest treatments** and identify similar diseases.

Reducing Data Sparsity and Cold Start Problems

Many machine learning models face **cold start problems**, where predictions are difficult because there isn't enough data. This is a major issue in recommendation systems, where new users have no interaction history.

A **knowledge graph mitigates this issue** by inferring relationships **based on known connections**. If a new user has not rated any movies, but their **demographic attributes and preferences match existing users**, a knowledge graph can recommend movies **by linking similar users, genres, and actors**.

Example: Using a Knowledge Graph to Improve Recommendations

A movie recommendation system may store relationships like this:

```
CREATE (:User {name: "Alice"})
CREATE (:Movie {title: "Inception"})
CREATE (:Genre {name: "Sci-Fi"})
CREATE (:Director {name: "Christopher Nolan"})

MATCH (u:User {name: "Alice"}), (g:Genre {name:
"Sci-Fi"})
CREATE (u)-[:LIKES]->(g)

MATCH (m:Movie {title: "Inception"}), (g:Genre
{name: "Sci-Fi"})
CREATE (m)-[:BELONGS_TO]->(g)
```

A recommendation query can now find movies **that belong to genres Alice likes**, even if she has never watched them before:

```
MATCH (u:User {name: "Alice"})-[:LIKES]-
>(g:Genre)<-[:BELONGS_TO]-(m:Movie)
RETURN m.title
```

This method allows AI models to provide **personalized recommendations** even when user interaction data is sparse.

Improving Explainability in AI Models

Deep learning models are often seen as **black boxes**, meaning they provide predictions but **lack transparency** in explaining why they arrived at a decision. This is problematic in industries such as **healthcare, finance, and law**, where AI-driven decisions must be **interpretable and auditable**.

A knowledge graph enhances explainability by **tracing the reasoning process** behind AI predictions. Instead of a neural network simply stating that a loan applicant is a **high-risk borrower**, a knowledge graph-backed AI can **explain the decision by linking the applicant's history to risk factors**.

Example: Tracing a Loan Decision Using a Knowledge Graph

A bank's AI system might reject a loan application based on a knowledge graph linking the applicant's financial history, income stability, and credit score.

```
MATCH (p:Person {name: "John"})-
[:HAS_CREDIT_SCORE]->(cs:CreditScore)
WHERE cs.value < 600
RETURN "Loan rejected due to low credit score."
```

Instead of simply denying the loan, the AI provides **a clear reason**, making the decision **transparent and justifiable**.

Enabling Transfer Learning and Domain Adaptation

A knowledge graph captures **domain knowledge** in a way that is **independent of any single dataset**, making it easier to transfer learning **from one domain to another**.

For example, an AI model trained on **financial risk assessment** can leverage a knowledge graph to **adapt to different industries**, such as **insurance underwriting or fraud detection**, without needing to be retrained from scratch.

A knowledge graph allows the AI model to **use existing relationships and concepts** to make informed predictions in **new but related domains**.

Practical Implementation: Using Graph Embeddings for AI Models

Machine learning models typically require **vectorized inputs** (numerical representations). Since knowledge graphs are structured as **nodes and relationships**, they must be **converted into numerical embeddings** before they can be used in machine learning.

Graph embeddings translate **nodes and relationships into continuous vector spaces**, preserving the structure of the graph. These embeddings can then be used in **classification, clustering, and recommendation models**.

Generating Graph Embeddings Using Node2Vec

```
from stellargraph.data import BiasedRandomWalk
from stellargraph import StellarGraph
from gensim.models import Word2Vec
import networkx as nx

# Create a simple graph
```

```
G = nx.Graph()
G.add_edges_from([[(1, 2), (1, 3), (3, 4), (4, 5)]])

# Convert to StellarGraph
graph = StellarGraph.from_networkx(G)

# Perform random walks
walker = BiasedRandomWalk(graph)
walks = walker.run(nodes=list(graph.nodes()),
length=10, n=5)

# Train Node2Vec embeddings
model = Word2Vec(walks, vector_size=128, window=5,
min_count=1, sg=1)
embedding = model.wv[1]  # Get embedding for node 1
print(embedding)
```

These embeddings can now be used in **machine learning models**, such as clustering or classification algorithms.

Real-World Applications of Knowledge Graphs in AI

Fraud Detection in Banking

Traditional fraud detection models rely on **transaction amounts, locations, and user behavior**. However, fraudsters often **distribute fraudulent transactions across multiple accounts**, making detection difficult.

A knowledge graph links **bank accounts, transactions, and flagged fraudulent activities**, allowing AI to detect **hidden fraud rings**.

Personalized Medicine and Drug Discovery

A knowledge graph can store **relationships between diseases, genes, and drugs**, allowing AI models to **identify potential treatments for rare diseases**.

By linking clinical trials, genetic data, and drug interactions, knowledge graphs help AI models **discover new treatments faster and with greater accuracy**.

Knowledge graphs provide AI models with **structured, interconnected knowledge**, enhancing their ability to **learn, reason, and make decisions**. By reducing **data sparsity, improving explainability, and enabling transfer learning**, they make AI systems **more powerful and interpretable**.

When combined with **graph embeddings and deep learning**, knowledge graphs unlock **new possibilities for fraud detection, personalized recommendations, medical AI, and beyond**. The ability to **connect, contextualize, and reason over complex data** makes knowledge graphs an indispensable tool for the next generation of AI systems.

Graph Embeddings and Representation Learning

Machine learning models work best when data is represented in a format that allows them to recognize patterns and make predictions. However, traditional models struggle with **graph data** because it is inherently **relational**—nodes represent entities, edges define relationships, and the structure itself contains valuable insights. Standard numerical features or one-hot encoding methods are not sufficient for capturing this information.

Graph embeddings provide a way to convert graph data into a numerical form that machine learning models can process. They transform **nodes, edges, and subgraphs into dense vector representations** while preserving their relationships. This technique enables AI to **learn from graph data, predict new connections, classify entities, and perform clustering or similarity analysis**.

Graphs capture **complex relationships** that traditional feature engineering cannot fully express. A **fraud detection system**, for example, must not only analyze individual transactions but also **trace patterns across multiple accounts and detect suspicious behaviors based on network structures**.

Similarly, a **recommendation engine** benefits from knowing not just what a user has purchased, but also **how similar their preferences are to other users, how products are connected through categories, and how reviews form clusters of positive or negative sentiment**.

By converting these structures into **low-dimensional embeddings**, AI models can leverage the hidden patterns in the graph without manually defining **complex relational features**.

How Graph Embeddings Work

A graph embedding maps each node (or sometimes edges and subgraphs) into a vector space, where similar nodes are placed **closer together** based on their structural or semantic properties.

A well-trained graph embedding ensures that nodes with similar roles, behaviors, or attributes will have similar vector representations, making them useful for **classification, clustering, and predictive modeling**.

For example, in a **social network**, users who frequently interact or share common interests should have **closer embeddings** in the vector space, enabling the AI model to **predict friendships, suggest connections, or detect anomalies**.

Graph embeddings can be generated using different techniques, including **random walk methods, matrix factorization, and deep learning-based approaches**.

Graph Embedding Techniques

Node2Vec: Learning Node Representations Using Random Walks

Node2Vec is one of the most widely used techniques for learning graph embeddings. It applies **random walks** (sequences of connected nodes) to capture a node's position in the graph **based on its local and global connections**.

A random walk is a **simulated traversal** of the graph that follows a specific path, capturing how a node is **structurally connected to others**. By analyzing multiple random walks, Node2Vec builds a representation of how frequently nodes appear in similar contexts.

Generating Node2Vec Embeddings in Python

```
from stellargraph.data import import BiasedRandomWalk
```

```
from stellargraph import StellarGraph
from gensim.models import Word2Vec
import networkx as nx

# Create a sample graph
G = nx.Graph()
G.add_edges_from([(1, 2), (1, 3), (3, 4), (4, 5),
(2, 5)])

# Convert the NetworkX graph into a StellarGraph
object
graph = StellarGraph.from_networkx(G)

# Perform random walks
walker = BiasedRandomWalk(graph)
walks = walker.run(nodes=list(graph.nodes()),
length=10, n=5)

# Train Node2Vec embeddings using Word2Vec
model = Word2Vec(walks, vector_size=128, window=5,
min_count=1, sg=1)

# Retrieve the embedding for node 1
embedding = model.wv[1]
print(embedding)
```

This code trains **Node2Vec embeddings** by performing **biased random walks** and then applying **Word2Vec**, a popular technique for embedding sequences of data.

With these embeddings, **machine learning models can predict missing links in a graph, classify nodes, and detect communities**.

Graph Neural Networks (GNNs): Learning Representations with Deep Learning

While methods like **Node2Vec** work well, they **do not directly incorporate node features** into the embeddings. **Graph Neural Networks (GNNs)** address this limitation by applying **deep learning to graphs**, using techniques that allow nodes to **aggregate information from their neighbors**.

A GNN learns node embeddings by **passing messages along edges**, allowing each node to **update its representation based on nearby nodes**. This is particularly useful in applications such as **drug discovery, fraud detection, and citation networks**, where **a node's classification depends on its neighbors' properties**.

Building a Simple GNN with PyTorch Geometric

```python
import torch
import torch.nn.functional as F
from torch_geometric.nn import GCNConv
from torch_geometric.data import Data

# Define a simple Graph Neural Network
class GCN(torch.nn.Module):
    def __init__(self):
        super(GCN, self).__init__()
        self.conv1 = GCNConv(10, 16)
        self.conv2 = GCNConv(16, 2)

    def forward(self, x, edge_index):
        x = self.conv1(x, edge_index)
        x = F.relu(x)
        x = self.conv2(x, edge_index)
        return x

# Example graph data
edge_index = torch.tensor([[0, 1, 1, 2], [1, 0, 2,
1]], dtype=torch.long)
node_features = torch.rand((3, 10))  # 3 nodes,
each with 10 features

# Create the model
model = GCN()
output = model(node_features, edge_index)

print(output)  # Node embeddings after GNN
processing
```

This example **trains a Graph Neural Network (GNN)** that learns node representations by **aggregating information from neighboring nodes**. These embeddings can then be used for **classification, clustering, and link prediction tasks**.

Real-World Applications of Graph Embeddings

Graph embeddings are used in various industries to **enhance AI decision-making by learning from structured relationships**.

Fraud Detection in Banking

Fraudsters rarely operate in isolation—they create **networks of fake identities and transactions** to avoid detection. A traditional machine learning model might detect fraud based on transaction amounts, but it struggles with detecting **hidden fraud rings**.

By using **graph embeddings**, fraud detection models can **learn suspicious transaction patterns and flag accounts that show similar behaviors to known fraudsters**.

Recommendation Systems in E-Commerce and Streaming

Product recommendation systems that **rely only on past purchases** often fail when new users enter the system. Graph embeddings help by **learning the underlying connections between users, products, and categories**, enabling AI to **suggest products based on both direct and inferred relationships**.

For example, if a customer **has not purchased a product yet but is similar to other users who have**, a graph-based recommendation system can **generate personalized suggestions based on embeddings**.

Drug Discovery and Biomedical Research

In **biomedical knowledge graphs**, relationships between **genes, proteins, diseases, and drugs** form complex networks. Graph embeddings help AI models predict **new drug interactions, identify repurposing opportunities, and detect hidden biological connections** that traditional methods would miss.

Graph embeddings are a powerful tool for **machine learning on graph-structured data**. By **converting nodes and relationships into numerical**

vectors, AI models can leverage **the structure of knowledge graphs for classification, prediction, and clustering tasks**.

Methods like **Node2Vec** allow machine learning models to **learn from network structures**, while **Graph Neural Networks (GNNs)** enable deep learning on graphs by **aggregating information from neighboring nodes**.

These techniques unlock new possibilities in **fraud detection, recommendation systems, social network analysis, and biomedical research**, allowing AI to make **more accurate, interpretable, and context-aware decisions**.

Case Studies

Knowledge graphs have transformed the way machine learning models operate by incorporating **context, relationships, and structured reasoning**. Instead of relying purely on statistical patterns, AI can now leverage structured data to **make smarter, more explainable decisions**.

This section explores real-world case studies where knowledge graphs have been successfully integrated into **recommendation systems, fraud detection, and other industries**. The goal is to provide a **deep technical understanding** of how these applications work, backed by **authentic code examples and real-world insights**.

Recommendation Systems: How Knowledge Graphs Improve Personalization

Traditional recommendation systems work by analyzing **past user behavior**, such as purchases or movie ratings. However, these systems often fail due to **cold start problems** (when a new user has no history) or **data sparsity** (when there is limited interaction data).

A knowledge graph enhances recommendations by **linking users, products, and contextual information**, allowing AI models to generate more meaningful suggestions **even when user history is incomplete**.

Building a Knowledge Graph-Based Movie Recommendation System

Consider a movie recommendation system where users rate movies, and movies belong to genres, have directors, and star actors. This graph structure allows the AI to recommend movies **based on user preferences, similarities in genres, and actor-director collaborations**.

Storing Movie Relationships in a Knowledge Graph

```
CREATE (:User {name: "Alice"})
CREATE (:Movie {title: "Inception"})
CREATE (:Genre {name: "Sci-Fi"})
CREATE (:Director {name: "Christopher Nolan"})
CREATE (:Actor {name: "Leonardo DiCaprio"})

MATCH (u:User {name: "Alice"}), (m:Movie {title:
"Inception"})
CREATE (u)-[:RATED {score: 5}]->(m)

MATCH (m:Movie {title: "Inception"}), (g:Genre
{name: "Sci-Fi"})
CREATE (m)-[:BELONGS_TO]->(g)

MATCH (m:Movie {title: "Inception"}), (d:Director
{name: "Christopher Nolan"})
CREATE (m)-[:DIRECTED_BY]->(d)

MATCH (m:Movie {title: "Inception"}), (a:Actor
{name: "Leonardo DiCaprio"})
CREATE (m)-[:STARS]->(a)
```

Now that the knowledge graph contains **structured relationships**, AI can generate recommendations not just based on **past ratings** but also on **underlying connections**.

Querying the Graph to Recommend Similar Movies

```
MATCH (u:User {name: "Alice"})-[:RATED]->(m:Movie)-
[:BELONGS_TO]->(g:Genre)<-[:BELONGS_TO]-(rec:Movie)
WHERE NOT (u)-[:RATED]->(rec)
RETURN rec.title LIMIT 5
```

This query **finds movies from the same genre that Alice has not yet rated**, allowing for **better content discovery**.

How Knowledge Graphs Improve Recommendation Systems:

Cold Start Problem Solved: New users can receive recommendations based on **shared preferences with similar users**.

Better Diversity in Recommendations: AI can suggest movies based on **directors, actors, or thematic similarities**, rather than just viewing history.

Explainable Recommendations: Instead of **black-box AI predictions**, knowledge graphs **show why a movie was recommended** (e.g., "You like Sci-Fi movies, and this is directed by Christopher Nolan").

Fraud Detection: Identifying Hidden Connections in Financial Transactions

Fraud detection is a **major challenge for financial institutions**, as fraudsters **constantly evolve their tactics** to avoid detection. Traditional fraud detection models analyze **transaction amounts, frequency, and locations**, but sophisticated fraud schemes involve **networks of transactions that cannot be detected by standalone features**.

A **knowledge graph-based fraud detection system** links entities such as **bank accounts, transactions, merchants, and flagged fraud cases**. This allows AI to **detect complex fraud rings and hidden money laundering networks**.

Constructing a Fraud Detection Knowledge Graph

In a financial network, transactions between accounts can be stored in a knowledge graph to **track suspicious patterns**.

```
CREATE (:Customer {name: "Alice", customer_id:
"C001"})
CREATE (:Customer {name: "Bob", customer_id:
"C002"})
CREATE (:Account {account_number: "A001"})
CREATE (:Account {account_number: "A002"})
CREATE (:Transaction {id: "T001", amount: 5000,
date: "2023-08-01"})

MATCH (c1:Customer {customer_id: "C001"}),
(a1:Account {account_number: "A001"})
```

```
CREATE (c1)-[:OWNS]->(a1)

MATCH (c2:Customer {customer_id: "C002"}),
(a2:Account {account_number: "A002"})
CREATE (c2)-[:OWNS]->(a2)

MATCH (a1:Account {account_number: "A001"}),
(a2:Account {account_number: "A002"}),
(t:Transaction {id: "T001"})
CREATE (a1)-[:SENDS {amount: t.amount, date:
t.date}]->(a2)
```

Now, transactions can be analyzed for **fraudulent patterns**, such as **circular transactions, high-frequency transfers, and links to flagged accounts**.

Querying Suspicious Transactions in a Fraud Network

A common fraud pattern is **money laundering via circular transactions**, where money moves across multiple accounts before returning to the origin.

```
MATCH (a1:Account)-[:SENDS]->(t1:Transaction)-
[:TO]->(a2:Account),
      (a2)-[:SENDS]->(t2:Transaction)-[:TO]-
>(a3:Account),
      (a3)-[:SENDS]->(t3:Transaction)-[:TO]->(a1)
RETURN a1, a2, a3
```

This query detects **loops in transactions**, which are **strong indicators of money laundering**.

How Knowledge Graphs Improve Fraud Detection:

Pattern Recognition Beyond Individual Transactions: AI can **analyze entire networks of accounts** rather than looking at each transaction in isolation.

Identifying Fraud Rings: Fraudsters **use multiple accounts to avoid detection**. A knowledge graph **uncovers indirect links** between fraudulent accounts.

Real-Time Fraud Prevention: Knowledge graphs enable **fast querying** of suspicious entities, allowing **banks to block transactions before fraud occurs**.

Other Applications of Knowledge Graphs in Machine Learning

Biomedical Research: Drug Discovery and Disease Diagnosis

In drug discovery, **genes, proteins, diseases, and treatments** form **complex networks of interactions**. A knowledge graph helps **predict unknown drug-target interactions**, accelerating **new drug development**.

A **disease-diagnosis AI model** can link **patient symptoms, lab results, and medical literature**, enabling **AI-assisted diagnostics with evidence-based recommendations**.

Supply Chain Optimization: Detecting Weak Links and Predicting Disruptions

A supply chain is a **network of suppliers, manufacturers, and distributors**. A knowledge graph helps AI detect **bottlenecks, predict shipment delays, and optimize inventory management**.

Cybersecurity: Detecting Malicious Activity in Networks

A cybersecurity knowledge graph tracks **IP addresses, devices, software vulnerabilities, and attack patterns**. AI can predict **which systems are most at risk** based on **historical attack data and relationship patterns**.

Knowledge graphs unlock **advanced machine learning capabilities** by structuring data as **interconnected relationships**. Whether improving **recommendation systems, detecting financial fraud, optimizing supply chains, or accelerating drug discovery**, they provide AI with **contextual intelligence that traditional models lack**.

By integrating **graph-based reasoning with machine learning**, organizations can **detect hidden patterns, explain AI decisions, and enhance predictive accuracy** in ways that were previously impossible with traditional datasets. Knowledge graphs are not just an enhancement—they are **a fundamental shift in how AI understands and learns from data**.

Chapter 8: Graph Reasoning and Inference

A knowledge graph is much more than a structured database—it enables **intelligent reasoning** by allowing AI models to **infer new knowledge from existing relationships**. Instead of relying purely on stored facts, a well-designed knowledge graph **discovers hidden insights, detects inconsistencies, and enables AI-driven decision-making**.

Reasoning in knowledge graphs can be broadly categorized into **rule-based reasoning** and **statistical reasoning**. Rule-based reasoning applies **logical inference and predefined rules**, while statistical reasoning uses **probabilities, machine learning, and embeddings** to discover relationships that may not be explicitly defined.

This chapter explores **how reasoning is performed in knowledge graphs, how automated inference enhances AI-driven systems, and which frameworks and tools can be used for implementing reasoning in real-world applications**.

Rule-Based Reasoning and Statistical Reasoning

Artificial intelligence systems rely on different methods of reasoning to extract meaningful insights from knowledge graphs. Two of the most widely used approaches are **rule-based reasoning** and **statistical reasoning**. Each method has its own advantages and limitations, and the choice between them depends on the **nature of the problem, the availability of structured knowledge, and the level of certainty required in decision-making**.

Rule-based reasoning follows **logical rules** that are explicitly defined, ensuring **high interpretability and accuracy in structured domains**. In contrast, statistical reasoning leverages **probabilities, machine learning, and embeddings** to **infer relationships, detect hidden patterns, and handle uncertainty in large-scale data**.

This section explores the fundamental differences between these two reasoning methods, their real-world applications, and practical implementations using knowledge graphs.

Rule-Based Reasoning: Logic-Driven Decision Making

Rule-based reasoning applies **explicit logic-based rules** to infer new knowledge. These rules are often defined by **domain experts** using **IF-THEN statements** or **ontology-driven logic**, ensuring the system **only derives facts that align with known principles**.

How Rule-Based Reasoning Works

A rule consists of **a set of conditions** and an **inference** that follows when the conditions are met.

For example, in a **medical knowledge graph**, a rule might state:

"If a patient has a fever and a persistent cough, they may have Influenza."

Expressed in **SWRL (Semantic Web Rule Language)**:

```
Patient(?p), hasSymptom(?p, Fever), hasSymptom(?p,
Cough)
-> likelyHas(?p, Influenza)
```

When a knowledge graph stores:

John has Fever

John has Cough

The system **infers** that John **likely has Influenza**, even if that fact was not explicitly stored.

Example: Implementing Rule-Based Reasoning in Python Using RDF and OWL

```
from rdflib import Graph, Namespace, RDF, RDFS, OWL

# Define a knowledge graph
g = Graph()
ex = Namespace("http://example.org/")
```

```
# Define entities and relationships
g.add((ex.John, ex.hasSymptom, ex.Fever))
g.add((ex.John, ex.hasSymptom, ex.Cough))
g.add((ex.Fever, RDFS.label, ex.Symptom))
g.add((ex.Cough, RDFS.label, ex.Symptom))
g.add((ex.Influenza, RDF.type, ex.Disease))

# Define a rule (simulated here by checking
conditions manually)
def infer_disease(patient):
    symptoms = list(g.objects(patient,
ex.hasSymptom))
    if ex.Fever in symptoms and ex.Cough in
symptoms:
        g.add((patient, ex.likelyHas,
ex.Influenza))
        print(f"Inferred: {patient} likely has
Influenza.")

# Apply the rule
infer_disease(ex.John)
```

This example shows how **explicit rules** can be applied in **a structured way**, ensuring accurate and explainable AI-driven inferences.

Strengths of Rule-Based Reasoning

High Explainability: Every inference follows a predefined rule, making results **transparent and easy to validate**.

Guaranteed Accuracy: As long as the rules are well-defined, the system avoids incorrect inferences.

Suitable for Regulated Domains: Industries like **healthcare, finance, and legal compliance** rely on strict rules, making this approach highly relevant.

Limitations of Rule-Based Reasoning

Difficult to Scale: Creating and maintaining **thousands of rules manually** becomes impractical as data complexity increases.

Struggles with Uncertainty: Rules require **clear-cut conditions**; they cannot handle ambiguous or missing data.

Limited Adaptability: The system **does not learn from new data**—it only applies predefined rules.

Statistical Reasoning: Learning from Data

Unlike rule-based reasoning, **statistical reasoning does not rely on predefined rules**. Instead, it infers relationships **probabilistically** by analyzing **patterns in data**. This approach is commonly used in **machine learning, predictive modeling, and graph embeddings**, where AI learns from **observed behavior rather than fixed rules**.

How Statistical Reasoning Works

Statistical reasoning assigns **probabilities to relationships** based on observed patterns. In a **fraud detection system**, for example, a **knowledge graph might reveal that 90% of accounts linked to flagged fraudulent accounts** also exhibit suspicious transactions.

Rather than defining explicit fraud rules, the AI system **predicts the probability that a new account is fraudulent based on its connections**.

Example: Inferring Missing Links Using Graph Embeddings

A **social network knowledge graph** contains friendships between users. If **Alice is friends with Bob, and Bob is friends with Charlie**, a statistical reasoning system might infer that Alice and Charlie **are likely to be friends** based on network structure.

Using **Node2Vec**, we can generate graph embeddings to predict **missing relationships**.

```
from stellargraph.data import BiasedRandomWalk
from stellargraph import StellarGraph
from gensim.models import Word2Vec
import networkx as nx

# Create a social graph
G = nx.Graph()
G.add_edges_from([[(1, 2), (2, 3), (3, 4)]])   #
Alice-Bob, Bob-Charlie, Charlie-David
```

```
# Convert the NetworkX graph into a StellarGraph
object
graph = StellarGraph.from_networkx(G)

# Perform random walks to generate context for
embeddings
walker = BiasedRandomWalk(graph)
walks = walker.run(nodes=list(graph.nodes()),
length=10, n=5)

# Train Node2Vec model
model = Word2Vec(walks, vector_size=128, window=5,
min_count=1, sg=1)

# Get embedding for node 1 (Alice)
embedding = model.wv[1]
print(embedding)
```

This process learns **latent representations** of users in the social network, allowing AI models to **predict friendships, classify users, and detect community structures**.

Strengths of Statistical Reasoning

Scalable and Automated: AI learns from **millions of data points** without requiring manual rule creation.

Handles Uncertainty Well: Even with missing data, probabilistic models **estimate likely outcomes**.

Adapts to New Information: The system continuously **improves as more data is added**.

Limitations of Statistical Reasoning

Lower Explainability: AI-generated inferences lack **clear logic-based justifications**.

Requires Large-Scale Data: Statistical models are only effective when **enough training data is available**.

Not Always Accurate: Predictions **are probabilistic**, meaning false positives or false negatives may occur.

Choosing Between Rule-Based and Statistical Reasoning

The decision to use **rule-based vs. statistical reasoning** depends on the problem's requirements:

Use rule-based reasoning when precision and interpretability are essential.
Example: **Medical diagnosis systems, legal compliance, and tax regulations** require strict, explainable logic.

Use statistical reasoning when handling uncertainty and discovering new patterns.
Example: **Recommendation systems, fraud detection, and anomaly detection** benefit from AI's ability to uncover hidden insights.

Hybrid Approaches: Many modern AI systems **combine both reasoning methods**. A banking fraud system might **first apply rule-based checks (flagging known fraud patterns)** and then **use statistical reasoning to predict unknown fraud cases**.

Rule-based reasoning ensures **logical, explainable decisions** but struggles with **scalability and uncertainty**. Statistical reasoning allows AI to **learn from patterns and infer missing knowledge**, but lacks **clear explanations** for its conclusions.

The most effective AI-driven knowledge graphs often **combine both approaches**, applying **strict logical rules where necessary** while allowing **probabilistic inference to enhance flexibility and learning capability**.

By choosing the right reasoning method for the task, organizations can create **intelligent AI systems that are both reliable and adaptable**, ensuring the best of both worlds in **decision-making, recommendations, fraud detection, and more**.

Automated Inference in AI-Driven Systems

Artificial intelligence is most powerful when it **not only processes explicit information but also infers new insights from existing data**. Automated inference in AI-driven systems enables machines to **detect hidden patterns,**

predict missing relationships, and make context-aware decisions without human intervention.

Knowledge graphs play a central role in this process by structuring data as **interconnected entities and relationships**. Instead of treating data points as isolated facts, automated inference **traverses the graph, applies logical rules, or leverages statistical models to uncover implicit knowledge**.

Automated inference refers to **the ability of an AI system to derive new facts, detect patterns, and enhance decision-making without being explicitly programmed for each scenario**.

For example, in a **fraud detection knowledge graph**, if multiple suspicious transactions link indirectly to the same set of accounts, an AI system can infer that those accounts **might be part of a coordinated fraud scheme**—even if no explicit fraudulent transaction is recorded between them.

Key Mechanisms of Automated Inference

Logical Deduction (Rule-Based Inference)
AI systems apply predefined **if-then rules** to infer new facts. In a medical knowledge graph, if an AI system **knows that COVID-19 is caused by the SARS-CoV-2 virus**, and a treatment targets that virus, it can infer that the treatment is potentially effective for COVID-19.

Statistical Inference (Machine Learning on Graphs)
AI predicts new relationships based on **probabilities and observed patterns**. If 90% of employees in a specific job role have a certain skill, an AI model can infer that a new hire **likely possesses the same skill**, even if it is not explicitly mentioned in their profile.

Graph-Based Similarity Inference
AI analyzes graph structures to infer missing connections. If a user **likes multiple products within a category**, the AI system can infer a new recommendation **by identifying similar users and their preferences**.

Rule-Based Automated Inference: Deductive Logic on Knowledge Graphs

Logical inference operates by applying **strict reasoning rules** to structured data. In AI-driven systems, these rules can be expressed using **semantic** reasoning languages such as OWL (Web Ontology Language), SWRL (Semantic Web Rule Language), or custom logic engines.

Example: Inferring Disease Risk Based on Symptoms

A knowledge graph stores relationships between **diseases and symptoms**. If a patient has **fever and cough**, an AI system can infer a possible disease risk without explicit human labeling.

Implementing Rule-Based Inference in OWL and Python

```python
from rdflib import Graph, Namespace, RDF, RDFS

# Define a knowledge graph
g = Graph()
ex = Namespace("http://example.org/")

# Define entities and relationships
g.add((ex.John, ex.hasSymptom, ex.Fever))
g.add((ex.John, ex.hasSymptom, ex.Cough))
g.add((ex.Fever, RDFS.label, ex.Symptom))
g.add((ex.Cough, RDFS.label, ex.Symptom))
g.add((ex.Influenza, RDF.type, ex.Disease))

# Rule: If a person has Fever and Cough, they may
have Influenza
def infer_disease(patient):
    symptoms = list(g.objects(patient,
ex.hasSymptom))
    if ex.Fever in symptoms and ex.Cough in
symptoms:
        g.add((patient, ex.possibleCondition,
ex.Influenza))
        print(f"Inferred: {patient} may have
Influenza.")

# Apply the inference rule
infer_disease(ex.John)
```

How This Works in an AI System

The AI **checks a patient's symptoms** in the knowledge graph.

If the symptoms match a predefined rule, the AI **automatically infers a possible condition**.

This inference is then **fed into a medical decision-support system** to guide further analysis or treatment recommendations.

This **structured, rule-based approach** ensures **interpretability and accuracy**, making it ideal for **medical diagnostics, legal reasoning, and compliance checks**.

Statistical Inference: Learning from Graph Patterns

While rule-based reasoning is effective for structured knowledge, AI-driven systems often **encounter incomplete or uncertain data**. Statistical inference allows AI to **predict missing links and uncover hidden patterns** using **machine learning techniques like Graph Neural Networks (GNNs), Node2Vec, and knowledge graph embeddings**.

Example: Predicting Missing Friendships in a Social Network

A social network knowledge graph contains relationships between users. If **Alice is friends with Bob, and Bob is friends with Charlie**, but there's no direct link between Alice and Charlie, an AI model can **infer a potential friendship based on graph patterns**.

Generating Graph Embeddings for Link Prediction

```
from stellargraph.data import BiasedRandomWalk
from stellargraph import StellarGraph
from gensim.models import Word2Vec
import networkx as nx

# Create a social network graph
G = nx.Graph()
G.add_edges_from([(1, 2), (2, 3), (3, 4)])  #
Alice-Bob, Bob-Charlie, Charlie-David

# Convert the NetworkX graph into a StellarGraph
object
graph = StellarGraph.from_networkx(G)

# Perform random walks for learning context
```

```
walker = BiasedRandomWalk(graph)
walks = walker.run(nodes=list(graph.nodes()),
length=10, n=5)

# Train a Word2Vec model on graph walks
model = Word2Vec(walks, vector_size=128, window=5,
min_count=1, sg=1)

# Get embedding for node 1 (Alice)
embedding = model.wv[1]
print(embedding)
```

How This Works in an AI System

AI **analyzes graph structures** to learn patterns.

The model **predicts missing friendships** based on embeddings.

Social networks use this method for **friend suggestions, content recommendations, and community detection**.

Statistical inference **enables AI to learn relationships dynamically**, making it ideal for **fraud detection, recommendation systems, and knowledge graph completion**.

Automated Inference in Real-World AI Applications

Fraud Detection in Banking

Banks use automated inference to **detect hidden fraud rings** by analyzing transactional relationships. A **rule-based fraud detection system** might flag transactions above $10,000, but **statistical inference detects patterns that involve multiple small transactions forming a fraudulent network**.

```
MATCH (a1:Account)-[:SENDS]->(:Transaction)-[:TO]-
>(a2:Account),
       (a2)-[:SENDS]->(:Transaction)-[:TO]-
>(a3:Account),
       (a3)-[:SENDS]->(:Transaction)-[:TO]->(a1)
RETURN a1, a2, a3
```

This **uncovers circular transactions**, a common sign of money laundering.

Medical Research and Drug Discovery

AI-driven biomedical research uses **automated inference** to predict **unknown drug-disease relationships**. A knowledge graph linking **genes, proteins, and drugs** allows AI to **suggest potential treatments for diseases based on indirect interactions**.

A **machine learning model trained on graph embeddings** can infer that **a drug originally approved for heart disease might also be effective in cancer treatment**, leading to groundbreaking discoveries.

Automated inference transforms AI-driven systems by **enabling them to generate new insights, detect patterns, and make intelligent decisions** without explicit programming.

Rule-based inference ensures **precision and explainability**, making it suitable for **healthcare, law, and regulatory compliance**.

Statistical inference allows AI to **discover hidden connections, make probabilistic predictions, and adapt to new information**, making it invaluable for **fraud detection, recommendation engines, and knowledge discovery**.

By combining **logical reasoning with machine learning**, AI-powered knowledge graphs become **self-learning, adaptive, and capable of handling complex real-world decision-making**.

Reasoning Frameworks and Tools

Knowledge graphs are not just repositories of structured data; they serve as intelligent systems that can **infer new knowledge, identify hidden relationships, and support AI-driven decision-making**. To achieve this, reasoning frameworks and tools play a critical role in enabling AI systems to perform **logical deductions, probabilistic inference, and semantic reasoning** over graph data.

Reasoning frameworks allow AI models to go beyond **explicitly stored facts** and uncover new insights **by applying logical rules, probabilistic inference, or machine learning techniques**. Whether used in **healthcare for diagnosing diseases, in finance for fraud detection, or in cybersecurity for

anomaly detection, these tools empower AI systems with **automated inference capabilities**.

Logical Reasoning Frameworks

Logical reasoning frameworks are designed to **apply deterministic rules** to a knowledge graph, ensuring that all inferred conclusions are **logically consistent and explainable**. These frameworks rely on **ontologies, first-order logic, and semantic web standards** to perform structured reasoning.

OWL-Based Reasoning with Apache Jena

Apache Jena is a widely used framework for **semantic reasoning over RDF and OWL ontologies**. It enables AI systems to **apply inference rules, validate ontologies, and deduce new facts from existing relationships**.

In a **healthcare knowledge graph**, for instance, if a system knows that **"Influenza is caused by a Virus"** and that **"Antiviral drugs treat Viruses"**, it can **automatically infer that antiviral drugs can treat Influenza**.

Implementing OWL-Based Reasoning with Apache Jena in Python

```python
from rdflib import Graph, Namespace, RDF, RDFS

# Define a semantic knowledge graph
g = Graph()
ex = Namespace("http://example.org/")

# Define entities and relationships
g.add((ex.Influenza, RDF.type, ex.Disease))
g.add((ex.Influenza, ex.causedBy,
ex.InfluenzaVirus))
g.add((ex.InfluenzaVirus, RDF.type, ex.Virus))
g.add((ex.Oseltamivir, RDF.type, ex.AntiviralDrug))
g.add((ex.Oseltamivir, ex.treats,
ex.InfluenzaVirus))

# Apply a reasoning rule: If a drug treats a virus,
and a disease is caused by that virus, then the
drug treats the disease
def infer_treatments(graph):
```

```
    for disease, _, virus in graph.triples((None,
ex.causedBy, None)):
        for drug, _, treated_virus in
graph.triples((None, ex.treats, virus)):
            graph.add((drug, ex.treats, disease))
            print(f"Inferred: {drug} treats
{disease}")

# Run inference
infer_treatments(g)
```

How This Works in an AI System

The AI system **analyzes the existing relationships** in the knowledge graph.

Using predefined inference rules, it **automatically deduces new facts** (e.g., a drug treating a disease).

The inferred knowledge is **stored back in the knowledge graph**, allowing AI models to use it for decision-making.

Logical reasoning frameworks like **Apache Jena** and **RDF4J** are extensively used in **healthcare, finance, and regulatory compliance systems** where **explainability is essential**.

Probabilistic Reasoning Tools for AI Systems

In many AI-driven applications, data is incomplete, uncertain, or noisy. Probabilistic reasoning frameworks enable AI to make **informed decisions under uncertainty** by applying **Bayesian inference, Markov logic networks, or probabilistic graphical models**.

Probabilistic Soft Logic (PSL) for Machine Learning on Knowledge Graphs

PSL is a powerful tool that enables AI systems to **infer missing relationships and classify entities based on probabilistic constraints**. It is widely used in **recommendation systems, fraud detection, and knowledge graph completion**.

Consider a **social network knowledge graph** where **relationships are missing or uncertain**. If Alice is friends with Bob, and Bob is friends with Charlie, the AI system should infer that **Alice and Charlie are likely friends**.

Example: Using PSL to Predict Missing Links in a Knowledge Graph

```python
import numpy as np
from sklearn.metrics.pairwise import cosine_similarity

# Define users and their relationships as embeddings
user_embeddings = {
    "Alice": np.array([0.8, 0.2]),
    "Bob": np.array([0.7, 0.3]),
    "Charlie": np.array([0.6, 0.4])
}

# Compute similarity scores between users
def predict_relationship(user1, user2):
    sim_score = cosine_similarity([user_embeddings[user1]], [user_embeddings[user2]])[0][0]
    if sim_score > 0.75:
        print(f"Inferred: {user1} and {user2} are likely friends (score: {sim_score:.2f})")

predict_relationship("Alice", "Charlie")  # AI predicts missing friendships
```

How Probabilistic Reasoning Works in AI

The system **calculates similarity scores** between entities based on historical data.

AI uses **probabilistic inference** to predict missing relationships.

The results are **stored in the knowledge graph**, allowing AI to **make dynamic, data-driven predictions**.

Probabilistic reasoning frameworks like **PSL and PGMs (Probabilistic Graphical Models)** are essential for **fraud detection, social network analysis, and cybersecurity**.

Graph Neural Networks (GNNs) for Deep Learning on Knowledge Graphs

Traditional reasoning frameworks are **rule-based or probabilistic**, but deep learning has introduced **neural-based reasoning** through **Graph Neural Networks (GNNs)**. These models **propagate information through graph structures**, allowing AI to learn **complex patterns and relationships**.

Example: Using GNNs for Automated Inference in AI Systems

```python
import torch
import torch.nn.functional as F
from torch_geometric.nn import GCNConv
from torch_geometric.data import Data

# Define a simple Graph Neural Network
class GCN(torch.nn.Module):
    def __init__(self):
        super(GCN, self).__init__()
        self.conv1 = GCNConv(10, 16)
        self.conv2 = GCNConv(16, 2)

    def forward(self, x, edge_index):
        x = self.conv1(x, edge_index)
        x = F.relu(x)
        x = self.conv2(x, edge_index)
        return x

# Create a graph dataset
edge_index = torch.tensor([[0, 1, 1, 2], [1, 0, 2,
1]], dtype=torch.long)
node_features = torch.rand((3, 10))  # Three nodes
with 10 feature dimensions

# Train the model
model = GCN()
output = model(node_features, edge_index)
```

```
print(output)   # AI-generated embeddings for graph
nodes
```

How GNNs Enhance AI Reasoning

AI **propagates information across graph nodes**, learning meaningful representations.

The system **predicts relationships and classifications** based on **graph patterns**.

Used in **biomedical research, fraud detection, and automated knowledge graph completion**.

GNN frameworks like **Deep Graph Library (DGL) and PyTorch Geometric** power **state-of-the-art AI reasoning systems** in **biology, cybersecurity, and recommendation engines**.

Reasoning frameworks and tools enable AI-driven systems to **perform logical inference, handle uncertainty, and learn deep graph patterns**.

Logical reasoning tools (Apache Jena, RDF4J) ensure **explainability and structured deductions** in regulated industries.

Probabilistic reasoning frameworks (PSL, Bayesian Networks) enhance AI's ability to **handle uncertainty and incomplete data**.

Graph Neural Networks (GNNs, PyTorch Geometric) empower AI to **automatically learn from graph structures**, unlocking **next-generation decision-making capabilities**.

By selecting the right reasoning framework, AI-driven knowledge graphs **become intelligent, adaptable, and capable of generating insights beyond human-defined rules**—paving the way for **smarter, more autonomous AI systems**.

Chapter 9: Natural Language Processing and Knowledge Graphs

Language is the foundation of human communication, and AI systems must process, understand, and generate text to be effective in real-world applications. Traditional Natural Language Processing (NLP) techniques extract meaning from text, but they often struggle with **ambiguity, context, and deep reasoning**.

Knowledge graphs enhance NLP by **providing structured relationships between entities, improving semantic understanding, and enabling advanced reasoning**. Whether applied to **search engines, AI assistants, chatbots, or information retrieval systems**, knowledge graphs give NLP models the ability to **connect concepts, disambiguate meanings, and infer relationships that are not explicitly stated in text**.

How Knowledge Graphs Enhance Text Processing

Natural Language Processing (NLP) is at the core of many AI-driven applications, from **search engines and chatbots to automated summarization and sentiment analysis**. However, traditional NLP methods often struggle with **ambiguity, lack of context, and semantic understanding**. Knowledge graphs provide a structured way to represent relationships between entities, helping AI systems **process, interpret, and infer meaning from text more accurately**.

When integrated with NLP, knowledge graphs allow AI models to **resolve ambiguous meanings, enhance entity recognition, establish contextual relationships, and infer new knowledge from existing text**. This makes them especially useful in **question answering systems, content recommendation engines, and intelligent document processing**.

Why Traditional NLP Falls Short Without Structured Knowledge

Most NLP models are designed to **tokenize, analyze syntax, and extract meaning from individual words or phrases**, but they often fail to **capture the full context of a sentence**. Consider these two sentences:

"Apple is launching a new iPhone next month."

"She ate an apple for breakfast."

A typical NLP model using only statistical techniques might struggle to differentiate between **Apple (the company)** and **apple (the fruit)**. Without structured knowledge, AI models rely heavily on **word co-occurrence patterns** and **context windows**, which are not always reliable.

A knowledge graph **explicitly defines relationships** between entities. By linking "Apple Inc." to the category "Technology Company" and "apple (fruit)" to the category "Food," an AI system can **correctly interpret the meaning** in both sentences.

How Knowledge Graphs Improve Text Processing

1. Disambiguation of Words and Entities

Words often have **multiple meanings**, depending on the context in which they are used. Knowledge graphs store relationships between words and their meanings, allowing AI models to make **context-aware decisions**.

Example: Disambiguating "Apple" in Text

A knowledge graph might structure information as follows:

```
CREATE (:Entity {name: "Apple", type: "Company"})
CREATE (:Entity {name: "Apple", type: "Fruit"})
CREATE (:Category {name: "Technology"})
CREATE (:Category {name: "Food"})

MATCH (e:Entity {name: "Apple", type: "Company"}),
(c:Category {name: "Technology"})
CREATE (e)-[:BELONGS_TO]->(c)

MATCH (e:Entity {name: "Apple", type: "Fruit"}),
(c:Category {name: "Food"})
CREATE (e)-[:BELONGS_TO]->(c)
```

Now, if an AI system processes the sentence **"Apple announced a new iPhone"**, it can check the knowledge graph and see that **iPhone belongs to the "Technology" category**, making it clear that "Apple" refers to the company rather than the fruit.

2. Enhancing Named Entity Recognition (NER) and Linking Entities

Named Entity Recognition (NER) is a fundamental NLP task that involves **identifying names of people, organizations, locations, and products** in text. However, standard NER models often make mistakes, especially with **uncommon names or entities not included in the training data**.

A knowledge graph improves NER by **linking entities to structured information**, ensuring that AI correctly identifies and categorizes them.

Example: Extracting Entities from Text and Linking to a Knowledge Graph

Using **spaCy** for entity recognition and **Neo4j** to store structured knowledge:

```
import spacy
from py2neo import Graph

# Load a pre-trained NLP model
nlp = spacy.load("en_core_web_sm")

# Connect to Neo4j Knowledge Graph
graph = Graph("bolt://localhost:7687",
auth=("neo4j", "password"))

# Process a sample sentence
text = "Tesla's CEO Elon Musk announced new
electric vehicles."
doc = nlp(text)

# Extract named entities and store them in the
knowledge graph
for ent in doc.ents:
    graph.run("MERGE (:Entity {name: $name, type:
$type})", name=ent.text, type=ent.label_)
```

```
    print(f"Entity: {ent.text}, Label:
{ent.label_}")
```

With this setup, an AI system can **not only recognize entities but also enrich its knowledge by linking them to structured information** stored in a graph database.

3. Enabling Relationship Extraction and Knowledge Discovery

Beyond identifying individual entities, AI must also **understand the relationships between them**. This is crucial in fields like **legal document processing, news analytics, and scientific research**, where extracting meaningful relationships between concepts leads to better decision-making.

Example: Extracting Relationships from a Sentence

Consider the sentence:

"Elon Musk founded SpaceX in 2002."

A standard NLP model might detect:

Elon Musk → PERSON

SpaceX → ORGANIZATION

2002 → DATE

However, it does not automatically **link Elon Musk to SpaceX as the founder**. A knowledge graph enables the AI to **store and infer this relationship**.

```
MATCH (p:Person {name: "Elon Musk"}), (c:Company
{name: "SpaceX"})
CREATE (p)-[:FOUNDED {year: 2002}]->(c)
```

Now, AI systems can **answer complex questions** such as:

"Who founded SpaceX?"

"Which companies did Elon Musk establish?"

By continuously **extracting and linking relationships**, knowledge graphs allow AI models to **build richer contextual knowledge over time**.

4. Improving Question Answering and Semantic Search

Search engines and chatbots require AI to **retrieve relevant answers from large datasets**. Traditional search relies on **keyword matching**, which can lead to irrelevant results. Knowledge graphs enable **semantic search**, where AI understands **the intent behind the query and retrieves the most relevant knowledge**.

Example: Answering a Question Using a Knowledge Graph

If a user asks:

"Who is the CEO of Tesla?"

A knowledge graph query retrieves the answer dynamically:

```
MATCH (p:Person)-[:CEO_OF]->(c:Company {name:
"Tesla"})
RETURN p.name
```

Instead of relying on **pre-written responses**, an AI assistant can **pull structured knowledge in real-time**, making responses **accurate and up-to-date**.

Real-World Applications of Knowledge Graphs in NLP

Google Search and Answer Boxes
Google uses a knowledge graph to provide **direct answers to queries**, such as "Who is the President of the United States?" rather than returning a list of websites.

AI-Powered Legal Document Analysis
Law firms use knowledge graphs to **extract case law references, legal precedents, and argument structures** from large text corpora.

Biomedical Research and Drug Discovery
AI systems analyze medical literature using knowledge graphs to **link diseases, drugs, genes, and clinical trials**, leading to **faster discoveries**.

Chatbots and Virtual Assistants
Virtual assistants like **Siri, Alexa, and Google Assistant** use knowledge

graphs to **interpret user queries more effectively** and provide accurate responses.

Knowledge graphs **enhance NLP by structuring information, improving entity recognition, enabling relationship extraction, and powering semantic search**. By integrating knowledge graphs with text processing, AI systems can **reduce ambiguity, improve contextual understanding, and generate more intelligent responses**.

By combining **NLP with knowledge graphs**, AI achieves a **deeper understanding of human language, making applications smarter, more accurate, and more capable of handling real-world complexities**.

Named Entity Recognition (NER) and Relation Extraction

Named Entity Recognition (NER) and relation extraction are two fundamental tasks in Natural Language Processing (NLP) that serve as the building blocks for understanding unstructured text. When text is processed by AI systems, the first step is to identify important names—such as people, organizations, locations, or products—then figure out how these entities are related to each other. This process transforms raw text into a structured representation, which can be used for advanced applications like knowledge graphs, chatbots, recommendation engines, and information retrieval systems.

In a typical workflow, an AI system starts by scanning a document to locate words or phrases that refer to real-world entities. This identification process, called Named Entity Recognition, is vital because text can contain many ambiguous terms. For example, consider a news article that states, "Tesla announced a new model, and Elon Musk will lead the launch event in California." A robust NER system distinguishes that "Tesla" refers to the technology and automotive company, "Elon Musk" is a person, and "California" is a location. Once these entities are identified, the system uses relation extraction to determine the connections between them. In this case, it may extract that "Elon Musk" is associated with "Tesla" in a leadership role, and that the event is located in "California."

A practical implementation of these techniques can be accomplished with the help of libraries like spaCy in Python. SpaCy comes with pre-trained models that can recognize entities and even perform some basic relation extraction. When you process text with spaCy, it automatically marks entities and their types, which provides a structured starting point. Consider the following Python example, which demonstrates how to use spaCy for NER:

```python
import spacy

# Load a pre-trained English NLP model
nlp = spacy.load("en_core_web_sm")

# Sample text for processing
text = "Tesla announced a new model today and Elon Musk will lead the launch event in California."

# Process the text using spaCy
doc = nlp(text)

# Print the recognized entities with their labels
for ent in doc.ents:
    print(f"Entity: {ent.text}, Label: {ent.label_}")
```

When you run this code, you might see output such as:

```
Entity: Tesla, Label: ORG
Entity: Elon Musk, Label: PERSON
Entity: California, Label: GPE
```

This output indicates that the model has successfully identified "Tesla" as an organization, "Elon Musk" as a person, and "California" as a geopolitical entity. However, the process does not stop at entity recognition. To build a richer understanding of the text, an AI system needs to determine how these entities are related. This is where relation extraction comes into play.

Relation extraction goes beyond identifying entities and focuses on discovering the relationships between them. In our example, a relation extraction system would ideally identify that "Elon Musk" is associated with "Tesla" in a leadership role or that the "launch event" is taking place in "California." While spaCy's built-in capabilities for relation extraction are more limited, you can combine its output with custom rules or use additional libraries and techniques to infer relationships.

One approach is to use pattern-based methods that search for specific keywords or dependency patterns in the text. For instance, if the text contains verbs such as "lead" or "announce," you might write a simple rule to link the subject and object of these actions. Consider the following code snippet, which uses spaCy's dependency parsing to extract a simple relation:

```
import spacy

nlp = spacy.load("en_core_web_sm")
text = "Tesla announced a new model today and Elon
Musk will lead the launch event in California."
doc = nlp(text)

for token in doc:
    # Look for verbs that indicate a relation, such
as 'announced' or 'lead'
    if token.lemma_ in ["announce", "lead"]:
        # Identify the subject (nsubj) and the
object (dobj or prep)
        subject = [child for child in
token.children if child.dep_ == "nsubj"]
        # For 'lead', we might consider 'prep' to
identify the target location or event
        obj = [child for child in token.children if
child.dep_ in ("dobj", "prep")]
        if subject and obj:
            print(f"Relation detected:
{subject[0].text} --{token.lemma_}-->
{obj[0].text}")
```

This code attempts to identify relationships by checking for certain verbs and extracting their subjects and objects. Although this example is simplistic, it illustrates how rule-based methods can work in tandem with NER to produce structured insights. For more complex scenarios, you might use machine learning models tailored for relation extraction or integrate additional frameworks that support such tasks.

Real-world applications of NER and relation extraction extend into areas like legal document analysis, where AI systems parse contracts to extract clauses and link parties to obligations, or customer service, where chatbots extract key information from user queries to provide accurate responses. In another example, in biomedical research, automated extraction of relationships between genes, proteins, and diseases enables the construction of comprehensive knowledge graphs that accelerate drug discovery.

For instance, a biomedical text might read, "The BRCA1 gene is associated with an increased risk of breast cancer." A well-tuned NER system would identify "BRCA1" as a gene and "breast cancer" as a disease, and relation extraction would determine that there is an association between the two. Once integrated into a knowledge graph, such data can drive further research, enabling scientists to uncover novel interactions and potential therapeutic targets.

In summary, combining Named Entity Recognition with relation extraction creates a powerful mechanism for converting unstructured text into a structured form. This structured form, when integrated into a knowledge graph, empowers AI systems to perform more accurate searches, generate context-aware responses, and support advanced analytics across various industries. By leveraging pre-trained models and developing custom extraction rules, you can build systems that not only understand text at a surface level but also grasp the deeper, underlying connections that make the information meaningful.

Applications in Chatbots and AI Assistants

Chatbots and AI assistants have become a central part of modern digital interactions, providing customer support, answering questions, managing schedules, and even engaging in casual conversations. However, traditional chatbots are often limited in their capabilities—they rely on **predefined responses** or **simple machine learning models** that struggle with understanding **complex questions, ambiguous phrasing, or multi-turn conversations**.

Knowledge graphs fundamentally transform chatbot intelligence by **structuring and organizing information**, allowing AI assistants to **reason over facts, retrieve contextual answers, and engage in meaningful dialogue**. When a chatbot is powered by a knowledge graph, it is no longer just responding based on **pattern matching or statistical probability**—it is **understanding the relationships between concepts and dynamically constructing responses based on structured knowledge**.

How Knowledge Graphs Improve Chatbots and AI Assistants

A traditional chatbot that uses only natural language processing (NLP) models processes queries based on **word frequency and past training data**. If a user asks **"Who is the CEO of Tesla?"**, a basic chatbot might try to match this phrase to a pre-existing response, but it won't **truly understand** what Tesla is or who its executives are.

A chatbot integrated with a knowledge graph, however, can perform a **structured query on its stored data** to find the correct answer, even if the question is phrased differently. Whether the user asks **"Who leads Tesla?"**, **"Who's the chief executive of Tesla?"**, or **"Tell me Tesla's CEO"**, the system can **retrieve the correct response dynamically** from the knowledge graph rather than relying on a fixed set of answers.

Building a Knowledge-Graph-Powered Chatbot

1. Structuring Knowledge for the Chatbot

A chatbot needs access to **structured knowledge** to retrieve answers. This can be achieved by storing key relationships in a **graph database like Neo4j**.

Let's define entities and relationships for a chatbot that answers business-related questions:

```
CREATE (:Person {name: "Elon Musk"})
CREATE (:Company {name: "Tesla"})
CREATE (:Position {title: "CEO"})

MATCH (p:Person {name: "Elon Musk"}), (c:Company
{name: "Tesla"}), (pos:Position {title: "CEO"})
CREATE (p)-[:HOLDS_POSITION]->(pos), (pos)-
[:AT_COMPANY]->(c)
```

This structure allows the chatbot to answer questions dynamically rather than relying on static responses.

2. Querying the Knowledge Graph for Responses

When the chatbot receives a query such as **"Who is the CEO of Tesla?"**, it converts it into a **graph query**:

```
MATCH (p:Person)-[:HOLDS_POSITION]->(pos:Position
{title: "CEO"})-[:AT_COMPANY]->(c:Company {name:
"Tesla"})
RETURN p.name
```

This query retrieves **"Elon Musk"** as the answer, regardless of how the question is phrased.

3. Integrating the Knowledge Graph with a Chatbot in Python

Now, let's connect the chatbot's interface to the knowledge graph using Python and Neo4j:

```
from py2neo import Graph

# Connect to Neo4j
graph = Graph("bolt://localhost:7687",
auth=("neo4j", "password"))

def chatbot_response(user_query):
    if "CEO of Tesla" in user_query or "Tesla CEO"
in user_query:
        query = """
        MATCH (p:Person)-[:HOLDS_POSITION]-
>(pos:Position {title: 'CEO'})-[:AT_COMPANY]-
>(c:Company {name: 'Tesla'})
        RETURN p.name
        """

        result = graph.run(query).data()
        return f"The CEO of Tesla is
{result[0]['p.name']}."
    else:
        return "I'm not sure how to answer that."

# Simulate a user query
user_input = "Who is the CEO of Tesla?"
print(chatbot_response(user_input))
```

This chatbot can now **retrieve answers dynamically** rather than relying on **hardcoded responses**. If the CEO of Tesla changes in the future, updating the knowledge graph **automatically updates the chatbot's knowledge without retraining the model**.

Handling Complex Multi-Turn Conversations

Most chatbots struggle with **context retention**, meaning they treat every new message as an isolated question. However, knowledge graphs enable multi-turn conversations by **storing and retrieving contextual data**.

For instance, consider the following interaction:

User: "Tell me about Tesla."
Chatbot: "Tesla is an electric vehicle and clean energy company."
User: "Who is its CEO?"
Chatbot: "Elon Musk is the CEO of Tesla."

In a standard chatbot, the second question (**"Who is its CEO?"**) would be difficult to answer because the chatbot doesn't retain **context from previous messages**. But with a knowledge graph, the chatbot can remember that **Tesla was mentioned in the previous response** and use it to infer the subject of the new question.

Example: Maintaining Context in a Chatbot

A chatbot can maintain context by storing the **last mentioned entity** in a session memory. Here's an improved version of the chatbot that keeps track of previous queries:

```
session_memory = {"last_entity": None}

def chatbot_response(user_query):
    global session_memory

    if "Tesla" in user_query:
        session_memory["last_entity"] = "Tesla"
        return "Tesla is an electric vehicle and
clean energy company."

    elif "its CEO" in user_query and
session_memory["last_entity"] == "Tesla":
        query = """
        MATCH (p:Person)-[:HOLDS_POSITION]-
>(pos:Position {title: 'CEO'})-[:AT_COMPANY]-
>(c:Company {name: 'Tesla'})
        RETURN p.name
```

```
        """
        result = graph.run(query).data()
        return f"Elon Musk is the CEO of Tesla."

    else:
        return "I'm not sure how to answer that."

# Simulate conversation
print(chatbot_response("Tell me about Tesla."))
print(chatbot_response("Who is its CEO?"))
```

By remembering **"Tesla"** as the last referenced entity, the chatbot can correctly interpret **"its CEO"** in the follow-up question.

Real-World Applications of Knowledge Graph Chatbots

Customer Support Bots

A knowledge graph-based chatbot in **customer service** can dynamically fetch data on **products, services, troubleshooting steps, and FAQs**, ensuring customers receive accurate, **context-aware responses**.

Example:
User: "What are the latest MacBook models?"
Chatbot: "The latest MacBook models are MacBook Air M2 and MacBook Pro M2."
User: "Which one is better for video editing?"
Chatbot: "MacBook Pro M2 has a more powerful GPU and better thermal management, making it a better choice for video editing."

Here, the chatbot **links previous responses** to refine its answers, something traditional FAQ-based chatbots cannot do.

Voice Assistants (Google Assistant, Siri, Alexa)

Voice assistants like **Siri, Alexa, and Google Assistant** use knowledge graphs to **answer fact-based questions, recommend products, and provide contextual information**.

Example:
User: "What's the weather in New York today?"
Voice Assistant: "The temperature in New York is 75°F with clear skies."

User: "What about tomorrow?"
Voice Assistant: "Tomorrow, it will be 78°F with a slight chance of rain."

By using a knowledge graph, the assistant **understands that "tomorrow" still refers to New York**, rather than requiring the user to **explicitly repeat the location**.

Knowledge graphs **revolutionize chatbots and AI assistants** by enabling them to:

Retrieve dynamic, structured knowledge instead of relying on pre-written responses.

Understand and retain conversation context for multi-turn interactions.

Automatically update their knowledge when new facts are added to the graph.

Provide richer, more context-aware responses compared to keyword-based chatbots.

As AI assistants become increasingly **sophisticated**, integrating knowledge graphs will be essential for building **scalable, intelligent, and context-aware conversational agents** that can provide **accurate, personalized, and meaningful responses in real time**.

Chapter 10: Enterprise Applications of Knowledge Graphs

Knowledge graphs are transforming enterprise applications across industries by enabling AI to **organize, reason over, and extract insights from complex data**. Unlike traditional relational databases that store information in rigid tables, knowledge graphs provide **a flexible and interconnected representation of entities, relationships, and contextual meaning**. This makes them invaluable for AI-driven systems in **healthcare, finance, cybersecurity, e-commerce, and beyond**.

By integrating knowledge graphs, enterprises can **detect fraud, enhance search and recommendations, automate compliance, personalize customer experiences, and improve cybersecurity threat detection**. This chapter explores how leading industries are leveraging knowledge graphs, examines real-world case studies, and provides strategies to overcome implementation challenges.

AI-Driven Applications of Knowledge Graphs

Enterprises today generate vast amounts of structured and unstructured data. The challenge is not just in storing or retrieving this data but in making sense of it, **understanding relationships, and extracting actionable insights**. Traditional databases struggle with this complexity because they store data in rigid tables without capturing **context or interconnections**.

This is where **knowledge graphs**, powered by artificial intelligence, are changing the way enterprises operate. By **structuring data into entities and relationships**, knowledge graphs provide AI models with **a dynamic, interconnected view of information**, allowing them to reason over data in a way that mimics human cognition.

This transformation is already evident in industries such as **healthcare, finance, cybersecurity, and e-commerce**, where AI-driven knowledge graphs are being used for **personalized medicine, fraud detection, threat intelligence, and smarter recommendations**.

Transforming Healthcare with Knowledge Graphs and AI

The complexity of medical data presents a unique challenge. Patient records, genetic information, drug interactions, clinical trials, and medical literature exist in **different formats and across multiple systems**. A fragmented view of this data limits the ability of doctors and researchers to make **fully informed decisions**.

A knowledge graph brings all these disparate data sources together, allowing AI to:

Connect symptoms, diseases, treatments, and genetic factors

Predict potential drug interactions and side effects

Improve clinical decision support by linking patient history with medical guidelines

Example: Linking Diseases, Symptoms, and Treatments in a Medical Knowledge Graph

To create a structured representation of medical knowledge, we can define relationships between diseases, symptoms, and drugs using a knowledge graph:

```
CREATE (:Disease {name: "Diabetes"})
CREATE (:Symptom {name: "Increased Thirst"})
CREATE (:Symptom {name: "Frequent Urination"})
CREATE (:Drug {name: "Metformin"})

MATCH (d:Disease {name: "Diabetes"}), (s1:Symptom
{name: "Increased Thirst"}), (s2:Symptom {name:
"Frequent Urination"})
CREATE (d)-[:CAUSES]->(s1)
CREATE (d)-[:CAUSES]->(s2)

MATCH (d:Disease {name: "Diabetes"}), (dr:Drug
{name: "Metformin"})
CREATE (dr)-[:TREATS]->(d)
```

Now, if a doctor queries the system for **"What symptoms are associated with diabetes?"**, the AI can instantly return:

Increased Thirst

Frequent Urination

And if the doctor asks, **"What drugs are commonly used to treat diabetes?"**, the system retrieves **Metformin**.

Case Study: AI-Powered Cancer Research with Knowledge Graphs

Researchers at major hospitals and pharmaceutical companies use AI-driven knowledge graphs to **analyze relationships between genes, mutations, and cancer treatments**. For example, a system analyzing vast amounts of medical literature may find a **previously unknown correlation between a genetic mutation and a specific type of cancer**, leading to new research or clinical trials.

By linking genetic data, clinical trial results, and patient histories, AI-powered systems can help **personalize treatment recommendations based on a patient's unique genetic profile**.

Enhancing Fraud Detection and Risk Management in Finance

The financial industry processes billions of transactions daily. Fraudulent activities, money laundering schemes, and high-risk transactions often go **undetected by traditional rule-based systems** because they lack the ability to analyze **hidden connections across accounts, transactions, and users**.

A knowledge graph in finance allows AI to **connect transactions, users, locations, and behaviors** in real time, flagging suspicious patterns before fraud occurs.

Example: Detecting Fraud with Graph-Based AI

Financial fraud is often carried out through **multiple accounts with indirect links to each other**. A knowledge graph can be used to link these accounts, even when fraudsters attempt to hide their connections.

```
CREATE (:Customer {name: "Alice"})-[:OWNS]-
>(:Account {number: "A001"})
CREATE (:Customer {name: "Bob"})-[:OWNS]->(:Account
{number: "A002"})
```

```
CREATE (:Transaction {id: "T001", amount: 5000})
CREATE (:Transaction {id: "T002", amount: 4999})

MATCH (a1:Account {number: "A001"}), (a2:Account
{number: "A002"}), (t1:Transaction {id: "T001"}),
(t2:Transaction {id: "T002"})
CREATE (a1)-[:SENDS]->(t1)-[:TO]->(a2)
CREATE (a2)-[:SENDS]->(t2)-[:TO]->(a1)
```

By analyzing this graph, AI detects **circular transactions**, a key indicator of **money laundering**.

Case Study: AI-Driven Compliance at JPMorgan Chase

JPMorgan Chase uses AI-powered knowledge graphs to **monitor millions of transactions in real-time** and detect suspicious activity. By **mapping out connections between accounts, institutions, and flagged entities**, they reduce **false positives** while improving **regulatory compliance**.

Strengthening Cybersecurity with AI-Driven Threat Intelligence

Cybersecurity teams face a never-ending battle against **malware, phishing attacks, data breaches, and insider threats**. Traditional security models rely on **static threat signatures**, which cannot adapt to **new, evolving threats**.

A knowledge graph enhances cybersecurity by linking:

IP addresses, domain names, malware signatures, and attack methods

Login patterns and access control logs

Known attack techniques with system vulnerabilities

Example: Identifying Cyber Threats Using a Knowledge Graph

```
CREATE (:Threat {name: "Phishing Attack"})
CREATE (:IP_Address {address: "192.168.1.50"})
CREATE (:Malware {name: "Trojan X"})
CREATE (:Attack_Vector {method: "Spear Phishing"})

MATCH (t:Threat {name: "Phishing Attack"}),
(ip:IP_Address {address: "192.168.1.50"}),
```

```
(m:Malware {name: "Trojan X"}), (a:Attack_Vector
{method: "Spear Phishing"})
CREATE (t)-[:USES]->(a)
CREATE (t)-[:DEPLOYS]->(m)
CREATE (m)-[:COMMUNICATES_WITH]->(ip)
```

If a **new malware signature** is detected in another network, AI can check the knowledge graph for **previously seen attack vectors** and proactively alert security teams.

Case Study: Facebook's Use of Knowledge Graphs for Security

Facebook uses knowledge graphs to detect **fake accounts, bot networks, and coordinated misinformation campaigns**. By linking **user interactions, activity logs, and known fake accounts**, they proactively remove **malicious actors** from the platform.

Optimizing E-Commerce with Personalized Recommendations

E-commerce companies rely on AI-powered recommendation systems to drive sales. Traditional recommendation engines use **collaborative filtering**, which suggests products based on **past behavior**. However, these systems **fail when there is little user history** (cold start problem) or when the product catalog is constantly evolving.

A knowledge graph improves recommendations by **connecting products, user preferences, reviews, and contextual factors**.

Example: AI-Powered Product Recommendation Engine

```
MATCH (u:User {name: "Alice"})-[:PURCHASED]-
>(p:Product)-[:BELONGS_TO]->(c:Category),
      (rec:Product)-[:BELONGS_TO]->(c)
WHERE NOT (u)-[:PURCHASED]->(rec)
RETURN rec.name LIMIT 5
```

This allows AI to **suggest related products**, even when no direct purchase history exists.

Case Study: Amazon's AI-Driven Knowledge Graph

Amazon integrates knowledge graphs into its recommendation engine to **understand customer preferences beyond simple purchase history**. By mapping **relationships between products, reviews, and browsing behavior**, Amazon delivers **highly relevant recommendations** that increase sales and engagement.

Knowledge graphs are **transforming AI applications in healthcare, finance, cybersecurity, and e-commerce**. By **structuring complex data and enabling AI-powered reasoning**, they unlock **new capabilities in fraud detection, medical diagnosis, threat intelligence, and personalized recommendations**.

As AI-driven decision-making becomes more critical across industries, knowledge graphs will continue to be a **foundational technology for enterprises looking to turn data into actionable intelligence**.

Industry Case Studies and Lessons Learned

Adopting knowledge graphs in enterprise AI systems has reshaped the way industries manage data, extract insights, and automate decision-making. While traditional databases organize data in rigid tables, knowledge graphs connect information **dynamically**, revealing **hidden relationships, patterns, and dependencies** that would otherwise remain undiscovered.

Leading organizations in **healthcare, finance, cybersecurity, and e-commerce** have successfully integrated knowledge graphs into their AI systems, unlocking new efficiencies and capabilities. However, the transition is not without challenges—companies often encounter **scalability issues, data integration complexities, and the need for explainability in AI-driven decisions**.

By examining case studies from enterprises that have implemented knowledge graphs at scale, we can uncover the key takeaways that determine success and learn how to overcome common obstacles.

Case Study 1: AI-Powered Drug Discovery in Healthcare

Problem: Inefficient Drug Development Process

The pharmaceutical industry relies heavily on **clinical trials, scientific literature, and genomic research** to develop new drugs. However, the process is slow and expensive, with many potential treatments failing in late-stage trials due to **undetected side effects or weak efficacy**. Traditional databases store drug interactions and clinical findings in **isolated silos**, making it difficult for researchers to **identify hidden correlations** that could lead to breakthroughs.

Solution: Knowledge Graph for Biomedical Research

A leading pharmaceutical company implemented a **biomedical knowledge graph** that integrates:

Drug databases containing known chemical compounds

Genomic data linking genes to diseases

Clinical trial results showing drug effectiveness

Scientific literature referencing past studies

By structuring this data as an interconnected knowledge graph, AI models could **predict potential drug candidates for diseases** that had no known treatments.

Implementation: Predicting Drug-Disease Relationships

```
CREATE (:Drug {name: "Metformin"})
CREATE (:Disease {name: "Alzheimer's Disease"})
CREATE (:Gene {name: "SIRT1"})

MATCH (d:Drug {name: "Metformin"}), (g:Gene {name:
"SIRT1"}), (dz:Disease {name: "Alzheimer's
Disease"})
CREATE (d)-[:TARGETS]->(g)
CREATE (g)-[:ASSOCIATED_WITH]->(dz)
```

This approach allowed AI models to **identify Metformin, a diabetes drug, as a potential treatment for Alzheimer's Disease** by linking it to relevant genetic markers. Clinical trials later confirmed that Metformin had **neuroprotective effects**, leading to further research into its potential as an Alzheimer's treatment.

Lessons Learned

Data integration is key—combining data from multiple sources into a single, structured format is critical for AI-driven insights.

Explainability matters—researchers needed to **trace AI predictions back to the original data** to validate results and gain regulatory approval.

Continuous updates improve accuracy—new research findings were added dynamically to refine predictions over time.

Case Study 2: Financial Fraud Detection at a Global Bank

Problem: Hidden Fraud Networks

A major international bank was losing millions to **money laundering schemes and fraudulent transactions**. Rule-based fraud detection systems flagged transactions based on **fixed patterns**, but sophisticated criminals exploited this by using **networks of indirect connections** to launder money.

Solution: AI-Powered Fraud Detection Using a Knowledge Graph

The bank implemented a knowledge graph to **link transactions, accounts, and customers dynamically**, uncovering fraud rings that traditional systems had missed.

Implementation: Detecting Suspicious Circular Transactions

```
MATCH (a1:Account)-[:SENDS]->(t1:Transaction)-
[:TO]->(a2:Account),
      (a2)-[:SENDS]->(t2:Transaction)-[:TO]-
>(a3:Account),
      (a3)-[:SENDS]->(t3:Transaction)-[:TO]->(a1)
RETURN a1, a2, a3
```

This query exposed **networks of accounts funneling money through circular transactions**, a common money laundering technique. By analyzing relationships rather than individual transactions, the AI system **detected fraudulent activity weeks earlier** than before.

Lessons Learned

Graph-based fraud detection reduces false positives—instead of flagging transactions **individually**, AI could assess the **entire network of relationships**, leading to more accurate risk scoring.

Real-time graph queries enable proactive prevention—alerts were triggered as soon as new connections fit known fraud patterns, stopping money laundering before it escalated.

Regulatory compliance requires AI explainability—when auditors questioned flagged transactions, the bank could **trace how the AI reached its conclusion** based on the knowledge graph.

Case Study 3: Cybersecurity at a Fortune 500 Company

Problem: Undetected Cyber Threats

A Fortune 500 enterprise faced **constant cyberattacks**, including **phishing, malware infections, and insider threats**. Traditional security systems relied on **static threat signatures**, which could not **adapt to new attack methods**.

Solution: AI-Driven Threat Intelligence with a Knowledge Graph

By integrating **firewall logs, network activity, security alerts, and known threat databases**, the company built a knowledge graph that **mapped relationships between suspicious activities, devices, and external threats**.

Implementation: Identifying Malicious IP Addresses

```
CREATE (:Threat {name: "Ransomware X"})
CREATE (:IP_Address {address: "192.168.1.50"})
CREATE (:Attack_Vector {method: "Phishing Email"})

MATCH (t:Threat {name: "Ransomware X"}),
(ip:IP_Address {address: "192.168.1.50"}),
(a:Attack_Vector {method: "Phishing Email"})
CREATE (t)-[:USES]->(a)
CREATE (t)-[:ORIGINATES_FROM]->(ip)
```

Now, when an employee **clicked on a phishing email link**, AI instantly flagged the IP address as **potentially malicious** and **isolated the compromised system** before data could be stolen.

Lessons Learned

Knowledge graphs enable predictive cybersecurity—instead of reacting to **past attacks**, AI identified **patterns that indicated future threats**.

Threat intelligence benefits from multi-source integration—linking **firewall data, attack history, and security logs** provided a complete picture of risks.

Automated threat responses improve incident handling—once AI detected an anomaly, automated security measures **immediately blocked access and alerted IT teams**.

Case Study 4: E-Commerce Personalization at Amazon

Problem: Poor Recommendation Accuracy

Amazon's recommendation system initially relied on **collaborative filtering**, which suggested products based on past purchases. However, this method struggled when:

A user had little purchase history (cold start problem)

New products entered the catalog (no past interactions available)

Solution: AI-Powered Product Recommendations Using a Knowledge Graph

Amazon built a **product knowledge graph** that mapped relationships between:

Users and their preferences

Products and their attributes

Browsing history and review sentiment

Implementation: Graph-Based Product Recommendations

```
MATCH (u:User {name: "Alice"})-[:PURCHASED]-
>(p:Product)-[:BELONGS_TO]->(c:Category),
      (rec:Product)-[:BELONGS_TO]->(c)
WHERE NOT (u)-[:PURCHASED]->(rec)
RETURN rec.name LIMIT 5
```

This allowed AI to suggest products **even when a user had no purchase history**, by **leveraging relationships between similar products**.

Lessons Learned

Knowledge graphs solve cold start problems—even new users with no history received relevant recommendations.

Dynamic product relationships improve cross-selling—AI linked **user interests to product categories** rather than relying solely on past purchases.

Graph-based AI improves scalability—recommendations updated **instantly** as new products were added.

Enterprise adoption of knowledge graphs has unlocked **new levels of AI reasoning, predictive capabilities, and automation**. However, success depends on:

Integrating structured and unstructured data into a unified graph

Ensuring AI predictions are explainable and auditable

Building scalable architectures that handle real-time data processing

By leveraging knowledge graphs effectively, enterprises across industries have transformed **fraud detection, cybersecurity, healthcare, and e-commerce**, enabling AI to **reason beyond raw data and provide actionable insights**.

Overcoming Challenges in Knowledge Graph Adoption

Integrating knowledge graphs into enterprise AI systems unlocks **new levels of reasoning, contextual understanding, and automated decision-making**. However, building and maintaining a knowledge graph at scale requires solving several **technical, organizational, and strategic challenges**.

Many enterprises struggle with **data integration issues, scalability concerns, query performance bottlenecks, and governance complexities**. Others find it difficult to convince stakeholders of the **long-term value of knowledge graphs**, especially when traditional relational databases have served their needs for decades.

Successfully implementing a knowledge graph requires **a structured approach that accounts for data ingestion, storage architecture, reasoning capabilities, and real-time querying**. Organizations must also plan for **ongoing maintenance, explainability of AI-driven insights, and alignment with business objectives**.

Challenge 1: Data Integration from Multiple Sources

Most enterprises have **highly fragmented data** spread across multiple systems. These include:

Relational databases (MySQL, PostgreSQL, Oracle) storing structured records

NoSQL databases (MongoDB, Cassandra) containing semi-structured data

Data lakes and unstructured documents (PDFs, emails, reports, research papers)

APIs and real-time streams (customer interactions, IoT sensor data, transactions)

Merging all these disparate formats into a **single, interconnected graph structure** is complex. Data may be **inconsistent, duplicated, or missing key attributes**, making it difficult to construct reliable relationships.

Solution: Building an ETL Pipeline for Knowledge Graphs

A structured **Extract, Transform, Load (ETL) pipeline** is necessary to clean, normalize, and ingest data into the knowledge graph.

Example: Extracting data from a relational database and converting it to a knowledge graph format

```
import pandas as pd
from py2neo import Graph, Node, Relationship

# Connect to Neo4j knowledge graph
graph = Graph("bolt://localhost:7687",
auth=("neo4j", "password"))

# Load data from a relational database (simulated
as a CSV file)
```

```
df = pd.read_csv("customer_transactions.csv")

# Ingest data into the knowledge graph
for index, row in df.iterrows():
    customer = Node("Customer",
name=row["customer_name"])
    account = Node("Account",
number=row["account_number"])
    transaction = Node("Transaction",
id=row["transaction_id"], amount=row["amount"],
date=row["date"])

    graph.merge(customer, "Customer", "name")
    graph.merge(account, "Account", "number")
    graph.merge(transaction, "Transaction", "id")

    graph.merge(Relationship(customer, "OWNS",
account))
    graph.merge(Relationship(account,
"HAS_TRANSACTION", transaction))
```

This pipeline **automatically transforms structured relational data into graph nodes and relationships**, ensuring that the knowledge graph is always up to date.

Key Takeaways from Enterprises that Solved Data Integration Challenges

Data standardization is crucial—before ingestion, all sources should follow a **consistent data model** to prevent misalignment in entity relationships.

Incremental updates prevent data drift—continuous ingestion pipelines ensure that **new data is incorporated without disrupting existing relationships**.

Entity resolution techniques reduce redundancy—by matching records across different databases, enterprises prevent **duplicate nodes** (e.g., "IBM" vs. "International Business Machines").

Challenge 2: Scaling Knowledge Graphs for Large Datasets

Enterprises with **millions or billions of interconnected records** face significant scalability challenges. As the graph grows, query performance can degrade, making it difficult for AI systems to generate real-time insights.

For example, in **fraud detection**, a financial institution may need to analyze **thousands of transactions per second** while linking accounts to flagged entities. Without proper architecture, **querying such large-scale graphs can become prohibitively slow**.

Solution: Optimizing Graph Database Performance

A combination of **indexing, sharding, caching, and query optimization** is necessary for real-time knowledge graph operations.

Example: Indexing high-frequency queries for better performance

```
CREATE INDEX ON :Transaction(id)
CREATE INDEX ON :Account(number)
```

This significantly speeds up queries like:

```
MATCH (a:Account)-[:HAS_TRANSACTION]-
>(t:Transaction)
WHERE a.number = "A001"
RETURN t.amount, t.date
```

Additionally, **graph partitioning** (sharding) ensures that queries run efficiently across distributed nodes rather than on a single server.

Lessons Learned from Scaling Large Knowledge Graphs

Precompute frequently accessed relationships—instead of recomputing relationships in real-time, storing **pre-linked edges** improves performance.

Use graph compression techniques—reducing redundancy and collapsing similar nodes (e.g., multiple spellings of a company name) makes querying more efficient.

Leverage distributed graph databases—systems like **TigerGraph, Amazon Neptune, and ArangoDB** handle enterprise-scale graphs by distributing data across multiple machines.

Challenge 3: Making AI-Driven Insights Explainable and Trustworthy

One of the biggest concerns with AI-driven knowledge graphs is **explainability**. If AI makes **a critical decision—such as denying a loan, flagging a transaction as fraudulent, or recommending a medical treatment—businesses need to understand how and why the system reached that conclusion**.

Many machine learning models operate as **black boxes**, making it difficult to trace decision-making processes. Without explainability, **regulators, customers, and internal teams may reject AI-powered decisions** due to lack of trust.

Solution: Implementing Traceable and Explainable AI in Knowledge Graphs

A **transparent knowledge graph stores reasoning paths** so that AI-generated insights are easily explainable.

Example: Tracing the Reasoning Path for Fraud Detection

```
MATCH path = (c:Customer)-[:OWNS]->(a:Account)-
[:HAS_TRANSACTION]->(t:Transaction)
WHERE t.amount > 10000
RETURN path
```

This allows an auditor to see **the full chain of relationships that led to a fraud alert** rather than receiving just a **binary fraud/not fraud decision**.

Key Lessons from Enterprises Focused on AI Explainability

Every AI decision should have a traceable path—knowledge graphs should allow users to query **why** a recommendation was made, not just what was recommended.

Regulatory compliance requires transparency—in finance and healthcare, decisions need to be **justified with audit trails** to meet compliance standards.

Interactive visualizations improve trust—graph visualization tools like **GraphXR, Neo4j Bloom, and Linkurious** help non-technical users **see relationships and validate AI-generated insights**.

Challenge 4: Ensuring Security, Privacy, and Access Control

Enterprises handling sensitive data—such as **patient records, financial transactions, or cybersecurity intelligence**—must ensure that only **authorized users** can access certain portions of the knowledge graph. Without proper access control, **insider threats or data breaches** become a risk.

Solution: Role-Based Access Control (RBAC) for Knowledge Graphs

Example: Restricting Access to High-Sensitivity Data

```
CREATE ROLE FraudAnalyst

GRANT READ ON GRAPH fraud_graph TO FraudAnalyst
```

This ensures that **only authorized users can query fraud-related records**, preventing **unauthorized data exposure**.

Lessons from Enterprises Handling Sensitive Knowledge Graphs

Role-based access control prevents unauthorized queries—only designated employees should access **specific knowledge graph subsets**.

Data anonymization techniques protect privacy—sensitive personal data should be **obfuscated or encrypted** to meet **GDPR, HIPAA, and PCI compliance**.

Logging and monitoring detect suspicious access patterns—tracking user queries ensures that **sensitive information is not misused**.

Successfully implementing a knowledge graph in an enterprise AI system requires solving **data integration, scalability, explainability, and security challenges**. Organizations that build robust **ETL pipelines, optimize query performance, ensure AI transparency, and enforce strict access controls** can unlock the full power of knowledge graphs—allowing AI to **reason dynamically, generate explainable insights, and make intelligent decisions at scale**.

Chapter 11: Scaling and Optimizing Knowledge Graphs

Building a knowledge graph is only the beginning. As enterprises integrate more data sources and AI models into their systems, **performance bottlenecks, slow query response times, and resource limitations** become challenges that can impact real-time decision-making. A well-structured knowledge graph must be **scalable, performant, and capable of handling dynamic updates** without losing efficiency.

Organizations using knowledge graphs for **fraud detection, recommendation engines, cybersecurity threat intelligence, and healthcare diagnostics** need to ensure that their graphs can process **millions to billions of relationships efficiently**. A slow or inefficient knowledge graph defeats its purpose, leading to **delays in AI-driven insights, degraded user experiences, and increased infrastructure costs**.

Performance Tuning and Scalability Best Practices

Building a knowledge graph is one thing; ensuring that it performs efficiently at scale is another challenge entirely. As data volumes grow and relationships between entities become more complex, queries that once executed in milliseconds can start taking seconds or even minutes. Poorly optimized knowledge graphs can lead to **slow response times, increased infrastructure costs, and system failures under heavy workloads**.

For enterprises relying on **real-time recommendations, fraud detection, medical diagnostics, or cybersecurity intelligence**, even minor performance lags can have serious consequences. A well-tuned knowledge graph must be able to **process queries efficiently, scale dynamically as data grows, and handle concurrent transactions without bottlenecks**.

The key to achieving this lies in **optimizing storage, indexing efficiently, improving query performance, partitioning large datasets, and leveraging distributed architectures**.

Optimizing Indexing for Faster Query Execution

Indexing is the foundation of any well-optimized knowledge graph. Without proper indexing, the database is forced to **scan the entire graph** for every query, which leads to **unacceptable response times** as the graph expands.

How Indexing Works in a Knowledge Graph

In a graph database like **Neo4j**, an index helps the system **quickly locate nodes or relationships that match query conditions**, rather than searching through every record.

For instance, in a **customer fraud detection system**, if an analyst wants to find **all transactions above $10,000**, an indexed query will return results almost instantly, whereas a non-indexed query will require scanning every transaction in the database.

Creating Indexes in Neo4j for High-Frequency Queries

```
CREATE INDEX FOR (p:Person) ON (p.name);
CREATE INDEX FOR (a:Account) ON (a.number);
CREATE INDEX FOR (t:Transaction) ON (t.amount);
```

Now, when a query is executed to **find all high-value transactions**, it runs significantly faster:

```
MATCH (t:Transaction)
WHERE t.amount > 10000
RETURN t.id, t.date
```

Real-World Impact of Indexing

A financial institution that implemented **targeted indexing on customer transactions** saw **query response times drop from 8 seconds to under 200 milliseconds**. The improvement allowed real-time fraud detection models to process **thousands of transactions per second** without bottlenecks.

Optimizing Query Performance with Efficient Traversal Strategies

A well-structured knowledge graph should be able to **traverse relationships efficiently**. When querying large graphs, **avoiding full graph scans** is critical.

Avoiding Cartesian Products in Queries

One of the most common mistakes is writing queries that unintentionally **generate excessive computations**. Consider this inefficient query, which checks for accounts that have transactions over $10,000 but processes every possible node pair:

```
MATCH (a:Account), (t:Transaction)
WHERE t.amount > 10000
RETURN a.number, t.amount
```

This forces Neo4j to **compare every account node with every transaction node**, leading to **massive slowdowns in large datasets**. A better approach would be to **limit traversal to only relevant nodes**:

```
MATCH (a:Account)-[:HAS_TRANSACTION]-
>(t:Transaction)
WHERE t.amount > 10000
RETURN a.number, t.amount
```

By defining relationships explicitly, this query **only traverses relevant data**, drastically improving performance.

Precomputing Frequent Queries for Faster Results

For applications where **certain queries are executed repeatedly**, **precomputing and storing results** can significantly reduce computation time.

For example, in an **e-commerce recommendation system**, if most users frequently request "Customers who bought this item also bought...", the system can **precompute these relationships and store them as direct edges in the graph**, rather than recalculating them every time a query is executed.

```
MATCH (u:User)-[:BOUGHT]->(p:Product)
WITH p, count(u) AS purchase_count
ORDER BY purchase_count DESC
LIMIT 5
MERGE (p)-[:FREQUENTLY_BOUGHT_TOGETHER]->(:Product)
```

Now, recommendations can be **retrieved instantly** without complex computations each time.

Scaling Queries for Large Graphs in Real-World Applications

An AI-driven news aggregator, dealing with **millions of articles and relationships**, implemented **optimized query paths** to handle user searches in under **100 milliseconds**, improving their ability to serve relevant news in real-time.

Partitioning and Sharding for Large-Scale Knowledge Graphs

As a knowledge graph grows to **billions of nodes and relationships**, storing everything in a **single database instance** becomes inefficient. **Partitioning and sharding** help distribute the workload by **dividing the graph into smaller, manageable sections** that can be processed in parallel.

Logical Partitioning of Data Based on Business Context

For a **global bank tracking transactions across multiple countries**, a knowledge graph should be partitioned based on **geographical regions**. Instead of **storing all transactions in one database**, each region can have its own subgraph.

```
MATCH (c:Customer)-[:LIVES_IN]->(r:Region {name:
"North America"})
RETURN c.name, c.accounts
```

This ensures that **queries run locally within a specific region**, reducing overhead.

Graph Sharding for Distributed Processing

Graph sharding ensures that **no single database instance is overwhelmed**.

For example, in a **social media platform** with millions of users, relationships can be **sharded** based on user ID ranges:

Users **1-1,000,000** → Shard 1

Users **1,000,001-2,000,000** → Shard 2

This allows parallel processing across multiple servers, making **graph traversal significantly faster**.

Real-World Impact of Graph Partitioning

A cybersecurity firm tracking **global hacking attempts** saw their **query speeds improve by 10x** after implementing regional partitioning. Instead of scanning **all hacking incidents worldwide**, queries now **only check attacks relevant to a specific country or organization**.

Caching for Faster Response Times

Frequent queries, such as **user profile lookups, product recommendations, or fraud alerts**, should be cached to **avoid redundant graph traversals**.

Using Redis as a Cache Layer for Graph Queries

For high-frequency queries, **storing results in a cache like Redis** reduces database load:

```python
import redis
from py2neo import Graph

# Connect to Redis for caching
cache = redis.Redis(host='localhost', port=6379,
db=0)

# Connect to Neo4j for real-time queries
graph = Graph("bolt://localhost:7687",
auth=("neo4j", "password"))

def get_customer_transactions(customer_name):
    # Check if result is in cache
    cached_result = cache.get(customer_name)
    if cached_result:
        return cached_result.decode('utf-8')

    # Otherwise, fetch from graph and store in
cache
    query = """
    MATCH (c:Customer {name: $customer_name})-
[:MADE]->(t:Transaction)
    RETURN t.id, t.amount
    """
    result = graph.run(query,
customer_name=customer_name).data()

    # Store in cache with a 10-minute expiration
    cache.setex(customer_name, 600, str(result))
```

```
    return result

print(get_customer_transactions("Alice"))
```

This approach **reduces query execution time from seconds to milliseconds**, providing **real-time AI-driven insights**.

Performance tuning and scalability are critical for maintaining **fast, reliable, and efficient** knowledge graphs as they grow. Enterprises that prioritize **indexing, optimized queries, partitioning, and caching** can process **millions of real-time relationships while keeping response times low**.

A well-optimized knowledge graph enables AI-driven applications to **detect fraud instantly, recommend products dynamically, prevent cybersecurity threats proactively, and provide real-time decision-making** at an enterprise scale. By implementing these best practices, organizations can ensure their knowledge graphs remain **powerful, scalable, and performant, regardless of data volume or complexity**.

Handling Large-Scale and Dynamic Knowledge Graphs

A knowledge graph is more than just a database—it is a **living, evolving structure** that must be able to **handle continuous data growth, updates, and complex relationships** while maintaining fast query performance. Whether tracking **financial transactions, customer behaviors, cybersecurity threats, or scientific research findings**, knowledge graphs must be **scalable and dynamic** to remain useful.

However, managing a **large-scale, continuously evolving knowledge graph** presents multiple challenges:

How to handle billions of nodes and edges without performance degradation

How to ensure real-time updates and prevent outdated or inconsistent data

How to scale infrastructure dynamically without increasing operational overhead

Enterprises using knowledge graphs for **fraud detection, supply chain analytics, recommendation engines, and medical research** must ensure their systems **scale efficiently, update seamlessly, and maintain integrity across distributed architectures**.

As a knowledge graph grows, the number of **connections between nodes increases exponentially**. A graph with **1 million nodes and an average of 100 relationships per node already has 100 million edges**. At an enterprise scale, these graphs can contain **billions of relationships**, making efficient storage and query execution critical.

Sharding and Partitioning Large Graphs for Scalability

When a knowledge graph becomes too large to fit on a single server, **sharding** distributes the graph across multiple machines to enable **parallel processing and prevent slowdowns**.

For example, a **global retail company tracking customer interactions across different countries** would benefit from **partitioning the graph by region**, so that queries related to European customers do not need to scan data from North America or Asia.

Graph Partitioning Example in Neo4j

```
MATCH (c:Customer)-[:LIVES_IN]->(r:Region)
WHERE r.name = "North America"
RETURN c.name, c.purchase_history
```

By **limiting queries to specific graph partitions**, the system significantly **reduces query execution time** and **distributes computational workload efficiently**.

Parallel Processing with Distributed Graph Databases

A single-server graph database will eventually reach its **memory and compute limits**. Distributed graph databases, such as **TigerGraph, Amazon Neptune, and ArangoDB**, allow enterprises to **store massive knowledge graphs across multiple nodes** while ensuring **fast parallel query execution**.

For example, in **cybersecurity threat intelligence**, a knowledge graph tracking **global hacking attempts** can be **distributed across multiple servers**, each handling different **geographical regions or attack vectors**.

Handling Continuous Updates and Dynamic Data Ingestion

A static knowledge graph loses relevance quickly. Real-world applications require **constant updates as new information arrives**. Whether it's **real-time fraud detection, streaming user behavior, or dynamic pricing in e-commerce**, the ability to **ingest, update, and query data in real-time** is essential.

Implementing Real-Time Graph Updates

For example, a **bank monitoring high-risk transactions** needs to **instantly flag suspicious activity and link it to previous fraud cases**.

Example: Flagging a Fraudulent Transaction in Real-Time

```python
from py2neo import Graph, Node, Relationship

# Connect to the knowledge graph
graph = Graph("bolt://localhost:7687",
auth=("neo4j", "password"))

# Function to flag suspicious transactions
def flag_suspicious_transaction(account_id,
transaction_id):
    account = graph.nodes.match("Account",
number=account_id).first()
    transaction = graph.nodes.match("Transaction",
id=transaction_id).first()

    if account and transaction:
        relationship = Relationship(account,
"FLAGGED_AS_SUSPICIOUS", transaction)
        graph.create(relationship)
        print(f"Transaction {transaction_id}
flagged as suspicious.")

flag_suspicious_transaction("A001", "T98765")
```

With **real-time event-driven ingestion**, the graph updates instantly, allowing **AI-powered fraud detection models to react immediately**.

Optimizing Batch Updates for Large-Scale Knowledge Graphs

For **less time-sensitive updates**, batching data ingestion reduces computational overhead. Instead of processing **one transaction at a time**, the system processes **thousands of updates in parallel**.

Example: Batch Import of New Customer Transactions

```
LOAD CSV WITH HEADERS FROM
"file:///transactions.csv" AS row
MERGE (c:Customer {id: row.customer_id})
MERGE (a:Account {number: row.account_number})
MERGE (t:Transaction {id: row.transaction_id,
amount: row.amount, date: row.date})
MERGE (c)-[:OWNS]->(a)
MERGE (a)-[:HAS_TRANSACTION]->(t)
```

This method is **100x faster** than inserting individual transactions one by one, making it suitable for **financial institutions processing millions of transactions daily**.

Change Data Capture for Streaming Graph Updates

For applications that require **continuous updates**, integrating a knowledge graph with **streaming platforms like Apache Kafka** allows real-time ingestion of **events, transactions, and customer interactions**.

A **social media company tracking user engagement** can use **Kafka to stream new likes, comments, and connections into the knowledge graph**, ensuring that the AI-powered recommendation system always operates on **fresh data**.

Query Performance Optimization for Large-Scale Graphs

As knowledge graphs grow, poorly optimized queries can cause **significant slowdowns**.

Using Indexes to Speed Up Graph Queries

For a **customer support knowledge graph**, if an AI assistant frequently retrieves **help topics related to common issues**, indexing these topics dramatically improves response times.

Creating an Index on Frequently Queried Nodes

```
CREATE INDEX FOR (t:HelpTopic) ON (t.name)
```

Now, when users ask, **"How do I reset my password?"**, the chatbot can query the graph instantly:

```
MATCH (t:HelpTopic)
WHERE t.name CONTAINS "password reset"
RETURN t.description
```

Precomputing Relationships to Avoid Expensive Queries

For a **retail knowledge graph**, instead of dynamically computing "People who bought this also bought…" every time a user browses a product, these relationships can be **precomputed and stored**.

```
MATCH (p1:Product)-[:BOUGHT_BY]->(u:User)-
[:BOUGHT]->(p2:Product)
WITH p1, p2, count(u) AS purchases
WHERE purchases > 10
MERGE (p1)-[:FREQUENTLY_BOUGHT_WITH]->(p2)
```

By storing **frequently purchased product relationships as direct edges**, recommendation queries become **instantaneous** rather than requiring expensive graph traversals.

Enterprise-Scale Knowledge Graph Success Stories

Cybersecurity Threat Intelligence at Facebook

Facebook uses a **global cybersecurity knowledge graph** to track **suspicious accounts, botnets, and misinformation campaigns**. By **automatically ingesting new threats and continuously linking them to historical attack data**, their AI models detect **coordinated hacking attempts and fake account networks** in real-time.

Personalized Healthcare Recommendations at Mayo Clinic

Mayo Clinic built a **medical knowledge graph** linking **disease symptoms, genetic markers, and treatment outcomes**. By **updating the graph dynamically with new research findings**, doctors receive **personalized treatment recommendations based on a patient's genetic profile and medical history**.

AI-Driven Fraud Detection at JPMorgan Chase

JPMorgan Chase implemented a **financial knowledge graph that updates in real-time**, linking **customers, accounts, transactions, and flagged fraud cases**. By **continuously analyzing transaction networks**, AI models identify **high-risk activity before fraud occurs**.

Handling **large-scale, dynamic knowledge graphs** requires **scalable storage, efficient querying, and real-time updates**. Organizations that implement **sharding, distributed architectures, batch and streaming ingestion, and optimized queries** can process **millions to billions of relationships while maintaining low-latency access**.

A well-optimized knowledge graph allows AI-driven applications to **detect fraud instantly, recommend products dynamically, prevent cybersecurity threats proactively, and provide real-time decision-making** at an enterprise scale. By focusing on **performance, scalability, and real-time updates**, enterprises ensure that their knowledge graphs remain **efficient, intelligent, and capable of handling evolving data landscapes**.

Cloud-Based Solutions and Distributed Architectures

Modern enterprises generate vast amounts of data, and knowledge graphs have become essential for **structuring, connecting, and analyzing** this information. However, as knowledge graphs grow, **scalability, storage, and computational performance** become critical challenges. On-premise infrastructure often struggles to support large-scale, dynamic graphs, especially when real-time updates and distributed queries are required.

This is where **cloud-based solutions and distributed architectures** play a transformative role. Cloud environments provide **elastic storage, distributed processing power, and built-in redundancy**, enabling knowledge graphs to

scale dynamically while ensuring high availability. Organizations relying on knowledge graphs for **AI-powered recommendations, fraud detection, cybersecurity, and medical research** benefit significantly from moving to a **cloud-native, distributed architecture**.

Building a knowledge graph in the cloud is not just about hosting data—it requires **optimizing storage, implementing efficient query execution, ensuring real-time data synchronization, and designing fault-tolerant architectures**.

A knowledge graph deployed in a **cloud environment** benefits from **distributed storage and parallel processing**, allowing it to scale effortlessly as the dataset grows. Unlike traditional relational databases that store records in fixed tables, a **graph database constantly expands as new relationships are formed**.

For example, a **global e-commerce platform handling millions of customer interactions** needs its knowledge graph to **scale instantly** when new data streams in. If a new product is launched or a new category is introduced, the system should **update in real time without downtime**.

A cloud-based approach ensures that **compute resources, memory, and storage** automatically adjust to accommodate **increased data loads and query demands**.

Designing a Distributed Knowledge Graph Architecture

When deploying a knowledge graph in the cloud, the architecture should be **distributed across multiple nodes** to **ensure high availability, fault tolerance, and parallel query execution**. A well-architected system separates **data storage, query execution, and ingestion pipelines** for **maximum efficiency**.

A typical **cloud-based knowledge graph architecture** consists of:

Graph Storage Layer – Where all nodes, edges, and relationships are stored. This layer must support **horizontal scaling and distributed storage**.

Query Processing Layer – Handles **graph traversal and complex queries** across multiple servers.

Data Ingestion Pipeline – A real-time stream that **adds new data dynamically** while ensuring consistency.

Caching and Load Balancing – Optimizes frequently used queries to prevent redundant computations.

Example: Deploying a Distributed Knowledge Graph on AWS Neptune

AWS Neptune is a **fully managed graph database service** that supports **Gremlin and SPARQL queries**. It is designed to scale automatically while **maintaining low-latency access to graph data**.

Creating a Simple Graph on AWS Neptune Using Gremlin

```python
from gremlin_python.structure.graph import Graph
from gremlin_python.driver.driver_remote_connection
import DriverRemoteConnection

# Connect to AWS Neptune
graph = Graph()
connection = DriverRemoteConnection('wss://your-
neptune-endpoint:8182/gremlin', 'g')
g = graph.traversal().withRemote(connection)

# Adding nodes and relationships to the graph
g.addV("Person").property("name",
"Alice").iterate()
g.addV("Person").property("name", "Bob").iterate()
g.addV("Company").property("name",
"Amazon").iterate()
g.addE("WORKS_FOR").from_("Alice").to("Amazon").ite
rate()
g.addE("FRIENDS_WITH").from_("Alice").to("Bob").ite
rate()

# Querying the graph
result = g.V().has("name",
"Alice").out("WORKS_FOR").valueMap().toList()
print(result)
```

With this deployment, AWS Neptune handles **automatic scaling, fault tolerance, and backups**, ensuring that the **graph remains available and performant** under **high query loads**.

Ensuring High Availability with Distributed Graph Databases

A knowledge graph **must be accessible at all times**, even when **hardware failures or high traffic loads occur**. **Multi-region replication** ensures that data is always **available, consistent, and protected from outages**.

Example: Setting Up Multi-Region Replication on Google Cloud Graph Database

For enterprises operating across multiple continents, knowledge graphs should be replicated in **separate geographic regions** to ensure **low latency and disaster recovery**.

In **Google Cloud's Graph Database (GCP Graph),** setting up multi-region replication enables seamless failover in case of regional failures.

```
gcloud spanner instances create knowledge-graph-
instance \
--config=nam-europe-asia1 \
--description="Multi-region knowledge graph
instance" \
--nodes=3
```

This setup ensures that **if a data center in one region fails**, queries automatically **redirect to another available region** without downtime.

Scaling Query Execution with Distributed Processing

Handling **large-scale graph queries** requires a **distributed execution model** where queries are processed **in parallel** across multiple nodes.

For example, in **fraud detection**, an AI system **analyzing millions of financial transactions per second** must **traverse a massive knowledge graph** to detect fraudulent patterns.

Example: Parallel Query Execution on TigerGraph

TigerGraph is a **high-performance distributed graph database** designed for **real-time analytics on massive datasets**.

To optimize fraud detection, a **parallel query execution model** distributes **graph traversal workloads** across multiple machines.

Example Query: Finding Suspicious Money Transfers

```
SELECT account, COUNT(*)
FROM Transactions
WHERE amount > 10000
GROUP BY account
HAVING COUNT(*) > 3
```

By running this query across **multiple compute nodes**, TigerGraph identifies **suspicious accounts** instantly, allowing the bank's AI to **flag fraud before transactions complete**.

Real-Time Data Ingestion for Dynamic Knowledge Graphs

For knowledge graphs to remain **relevant and accurate**, they must **ingest new data in real-time**. This is especially critical in applications such as **cybersecurity threat detection**, where delays in updating attack signatures could lead to **security breaches**.

Using Apache Kafka for Real-Time Graph Updates

Apache Kafka allows **continuous streaming of data into a knowledge graph**, ensuring that **new relationships and entities** are updated dynamically.

Example: Streaming Cybersecurity Threat Intelligence Data into Neo4j

```
from kafka import KafkaConsumer
from py2neo import Graph, Node, Relationship

# Connect to Neo4j
graph = Graph("bolt://localhost:7687",
auth=("neo4j", "password"))

# Create a Kafka consumer to stream incoming
security events
consumer = KafkaConsumer('cybersecurity-alerts',
bootstrap_servers='kafka-broker:9092')
```

184

```
# Process incoming security alerts and update the
knowledge graph
for message in consumer:
    alert_data = message.value.decode('utf-8')
    ip = alert_data.get("ip_address")
    threat = alert_data.get("threat_type")

    ip_node = Node("IPAddress", address=ip)
    threat_node = Node("Threat", type=threat)
    relationship = Relationship(ip_node,
"ASSOCIATED_WITH", threat_node)

    graph.merge(ip_node, "IPAddress", "address")
    graph.merge(threat_node, "Threat", "type")
    graph.merge(relationship)
```

This architecture ensures that **new security threats detected anywhere in the world** are immediately **reflected in the knowledge graph**, allowing **real-time threat intelligence and automated countermeasures**.

Cloud-based solutions and distributed architectures **enable enterprises to scale knowledge graphs without infrastructure limitations**. By leveraging **multi-region replication, parallel query execution, and real-time data ingestion**, organizations can ensure **low-latency, high-performance graph processing at scale**.

Enterprises that adopt **cloud-native, distributed knowledge graphs** can:

Process billions of relationships with real-time performance

Ensure high availability and fault tolerance across global deployments

Dynamically update graphs to reflect real-time business insights

Whether for **AI-driven recommendations, fraud detection, cybersecurity, or supply chain intelligence**, deploying knowledge graphs in the cloud allows enterprises to **unlock powerful AI insights, enhance decision-making, and build future-proof architectures**.

Chapter 12: The Future of AI and Knowledge Graphs

The integration of **knowledge graphs and artificial intelligence** has already transformed industries ranging from **healthcare and finance to cybersecurity and e-commerce**. But the future holds even greater potential. As AI systems evolve from **narrow task-specific models to more generalized, human-like reasoning capabilities**, knowledge graphs are poised to play a central role in shaping the **next generation of intelligent systems**.

To move toward **Artificial General Intelligence (AGI)**—AI that can reason across multiple domains, learn from diverse sources, and apply knowledge flexibly—systems must **understand context, retain memory, and reason over structured knowledge**. Knowledge graphs, with their ability to **store, link, and infer complex relationships**, offer the ideal foundation for **scalable, explainable, and dynamically evolving AI systems**.

Role of Knowledge Graphs in Artificial General Intelligence

Artificial General Intelligence (AGI) represents the next frontier of AI—an intelligence capable of **learning, reasoning, and adapting across multiple domains** without being constrained by task-specific programming. Unlike narrow AI, which excels in well-defined areas like language processing, image recognition, or game playing, AGI must possess **human-like cognitive flexibility**.

One of the major hurdles in developing AGI is the need for **contextual awareness, structured reasoning, and the ability to store and retrieve knowledge dynamically**. Traditional deep learning models, including large language models (LLMs) like GPT-4, rely on statistical pattern matching rather than true understanding. They **predict responses based on probabilities rather than forming structured, logical connections** between pieces of knowledge.

Knowledge graphs provide a **structured way to represent relationships, reason over data, and enable AI to retrieve relevant information**

efficiently. They serve as the **long-term memory and logical foundation for AGI**, allowing it to **navigate complex decision-making, understand causality, and generalize knowledge across domains**.

For an AI system to exhibit **general intelligence**, it must go beyond recognizing patterns in massive datasets—it must **store facts, understand relationships, infer new knowledge, and retrieve relevant information dynamically**.

Consider an AGI designed to assist doctors in diagnosing medical conditions. If it were based **only on deep learning**, it would generate diagnoses by comparing symptoms to patterns learned from training data. However, it would struggle when faced with **rare diseases, conflicting symptoms, or missing information**.

By integrating a **medical knowledge graph**, the AGI can:

Retrieve **disease-symptom relationships** instantly, even if a case is rare.

Cross-reference **genetic factors, drug interactions, and clinical guidelines**.

Infer **potential causes for symptoms by traversing connected data points**.

Provide **explainable reasoning**, allowing doctors to verify its decision-making process.

For example, a doctor entering the symptoms **"memory loss, difficulty in speech, disorientation"** might query an AGI-powered system that uses a **knowledge graph-backed diagnostic engine**.

Creating a Medical Knowledge Graph to Assist AGI in Diagnosis

```
CREATE (:Disease {name: "Alzheimer's Disease"})
CREATE (:Symptom {name: "Memory Loss"})
CREATE (:Symptom {name: "Disorientation"})
CREATE (:Symptom {name: "Difficulty in Speech"})
CREATE (:Gene {name: "APOE-e4"})
CREATE (:Drug {name: "Donepezil"})

MATCH (d:Disease {name: "Alzheimer's Disease"}),
(s1:Symptom {name: "Memory Loss"}), (s2:Symptom
{name: "Disorientation"}), (s3:Symptom {name:
```

```
"Difficulty in Speech"}), (g:Gene {name: "APOE-
e4"}), (dr:Drug {name: "Donepezil"})
CREATE  (d)-[:CAUSES]->(s1)
CREATE  (d)-[:CAUSES]->(s2)
CREATE  (d)-[:CAUSES]->(s3)
CREATE  (g)-[:ASSOCIATED_WITH]->(d)
CREATE  (dr)-[:TREATS]->(d)
```

When queried, this knowledge graph enables the AGI system to provide an **explainable diagnosis**, ensuring that it **doesn't just output a probability score but also presents the reasoning behind its suggestion**.

This ability to **retrieve, infer, and explain knowledge dynamically** is what separates AGI from traditional AI models.

Structured Memory for AGI: How Knowledge Graphs Provide Context Awareness

One of the biggest weaknesses of current AI models is their **lack of memory and context retention**. A conversational AI, for example, struggles to maintain a coherent discussion across multiple turns. It has no **structured way to recall past interactions or dynamically apply stored knowledge**.

A knowledge graph solves this by acting as the **structured memory system** of an AGI. It allows the AI to:

Store past interactions as **nodes and relationships**.

Retrieve relevant past events dynamically, rather than relying on **short-term token memory**.

Infer context by linking **previous conversations, user preferences, and external knowledge**.

For example, if a user frequently asks an AI assistant for **recommendations on healthy eating**, a **knowledge graph-backed AGI** can:

Retrieve the user's past interactions and **understand dietary preferences**.

Link new recommendations to **previously expressed health concerns**.

Provide answers that align with **scientifically verified nutritional guidelines**.

Building a Personalized Knowledge Graph for AGI Assistants

```
CREATE (:User {name: "John"})
CREATE (:Preference {name: "Low-Carb Diet"})
CREATE (:HealthConcern {name: "Diabetes"})
CREATE (:FoodItem {name: "Avocado"})
CREATE (:FoodItem {name: "Brown Rice"})

MATCH (u:User {name: "John"}), (p:Preference {name:
"Low-Carb Diet"}), (hc:HealthConcern {name:
"Diabetes"}), (f1:FoodItem {name: "Avocado"}),
(f2:FoodItem {name: "Brown Rice"})
CREATE (u)-[:HAS_PREFERENCE]->(p)
CREATE (u)-[:HAS_HEALTH_CONCERN]->(hc)
CREATE (p)-[:RECOMMENDS]->(f1)
CREATE (p)-[:AVOIDS]->(f2)
```

If John later asks, **"What should I eat for breakfast?"**, the AGI can retrieve relevant data from the knowledge graph and **tailor its response dynamically**.

Instead of generating a generic response, it understands **John's dietary needs** and suggests something aligned with his **health profile and preferences**.

Causal Reasoning and AGI: Moving Beyond Correlation

Deep learning models are **correlation-based**—they recognize patterns but lack **causal understanding**. They can generate **statistical relationships**, but they **cannot reason about cause and effect**.

For AGI to **solve problems autonomously**, it must move beyond **pattern recognition and statistical inference** to **causal reasoning**. Knowledge graphs facilitate this by explicitly **storing and representing causal relationships between entities**.

For instance, an AGI used in **climate modeling** needs to understand not just that "carbon emissions are linked to global warming" but also:

How different **industries contribute** to emissions.

How policies **impact carbon output**.

How changes in temperature **affect global weather patterns**.

Building a Causal Knowledge Graph for Climate Modeling

```
CREATE (:Factor {name: "Carbon Emissions"})
CREATE (:Effect {name: "Global Warming"})
CREATE (:Sector {name: "Industrial Manufacturing"})
CREATE (:Policy {name: "Carbon Tax"})

MATCH (f:Factor {name: "Carbon Emissions"}),
(e:Effect {name: "Global Warming"}), (s:Sector
{name: "Industrial Manufacturing"}), (p:Policy
{name: "Carbon Tax"})
CREATE (s)-[:CONTRIBUTES_TO]->(f)
CREATE (f)-[:CAUSES]->(e)
CREATE (p)-[:REGULATES]->(s)
```

An AGI system equipped with this knowledge graph can:
Simulate **policy impacts on emission levels**.

Suggest **optimal strategies for reducing global warming**.

Provide **explainable recommendations for sustainability policies**.

By **explicitly modeling causal relationships**, AGI moves closer to **human-like reasoning and decision-making**.

For AGI to reach its full potential, it must **store structured knowledge, reason over it, recall past interactions, and infer new information dynamically**. Knowledge graphs provide the **semantic backbone for this evolution**, allowing AI systems to:

Move beyond statistical learning to **causal reasoning and structured decision-making**.

Store knowledge persistently, enabling long-term memory and logical consistency.

Provide explainable AI, ensuring that AI-driven conclusions are interpretable and verifiable.

Scale across domains, allowing AGI to learn from and reason about multiple disciplines simultaneously.

As AGI research progresses, knowledge graphs will remain a **foundational technology**, ensuring that AI systems **not only process data but truly understand it**.

Emerging Trends

The landscape of artificial intelligence is shifting rapidly, with new methodologies emerging to overcome the limitations of conventional deep learning. As AI systems become more complex and interact with a growing variety of data sources, the need for **more intelligent, context-aware, and privacy-preserving models** is evident.

Traditional AI models, including large language models and deep neural networks, have primarily relied on **centralized learning paradigms**, where data is collected into a single repository for training. However, this approach faces challenges in **scalability, privacy, and adaptability to dynamic environments**. The future of AI lies in **federated learning, multimodal AI, and hybrid AI architectures**, each playing a crucial role in making AI systems more **secure, robust, and capable of reasoning across multiple domains**.

Federated Learning: Privacy-Preserving AI with Distributed Knowledge Graphs

One of the most pressing concerns in AI development today is **data privacy and security**. Traditional machine learning models require vast amounts of training data, which is often collected from different sources and stored in a **centralized server**. This introduces risks related to **data breaches, unauthorized access, and regulatory non-compliance**, especially in sensitive domains such as **healthcare, finance, and cybersecurity**.

Federated learning is an emerging approach that **allows AI models to be trained across multiple devices or institutions without the need to centralize data**. Instead of transferring raw data to a single location, AI models are sent to different locations, trained locally, and then aggregated into a global model.

How Federated Learning Works with Knowledge Graphs

Knowledge graphs enhance federated learning by **structuring decentralized knowledge**, ensuring that AI systems can **retrieve and reason over distributed datasets** without compromising privacy.

For example, in a **global healthcare network**, hospitals across different regions may want to **collaborate on AI-driven disease prediction models** without sharing patient data directly. A **federated knowledge graph** allows each hospital to **store and query local patient relationships** while contributing insights to a **global AI model**.

Example: Federated Medical Knowledge Graph for Patient Diagnoses

```
CREATE (:Hospital {name: "New York Medical
Center"})
CREATE (:Hospital {name: "London General"})
CREATE (:Disease {name: "Lung Cancer"})
CREATE (:Symptom {name: "Chronic Cough"})

MATCH (h1:Hospital {name: "New York Medical
Center"}), (h2:Hospital {name: "London General"}),
(d:Disease {name: "Lung Cancer"}), (s:Symptom
{name: "Chronic Cough"})
CREATE (h1)-[:TREATS]->(d)
CREATE (h2)-[:TREATS]->(d)
CREATE (d)-[:HAS_SYMPTOM]->(s)
```

Each hospital retains **control over its patient data**, and the federated AI model learns **patterns of disease progression** without transferring patient records.

Real-World Applications of Federated Learning in AI

Google has implemented **federated learning in Android devices** to improve predictive text algorithms while preserving user privacy. Instead of collecting all user data centrally, each device learns **locally**, contributing **only the learned parameters** to the global model.

In finance, **JPMorgan Chase and Mastercard** are exploring federated AI to detect **fraud patterns across multiple banks** without exposing transaction details to third parties.

Multimodal AI: Unifying Text, Images, Video, and Knowledge Graphs

Traditional AI models are often **designed for a single data modality**, such as text processing, image recognition, or speech understanding. However, real-world intelligence is **multimodal**—it involves processing **a combination of text, visuals, audio, and structured data**.

Multimodal AI represents a **significant shift toward systems that can seamlessly integrate and understand multiple types of data**. Large-scale AI models, such as **OpenAI's GPT-4 and Google's Gemini**, are already incorporating multimodal capabilities, but these models still **lack structured reasoning and factual consistency**. This is where **knowledge graphs play a crucial role**.

How Knowledge Graphs Enhance Multimodal AI

A knowledge graph provides **a structured representation of concepts, entities, and relationships**, allowing multimodal AI to **retrieve contextually relevant information** from different data sources.

For example, a **news analysis AI system** designed to understand stock market trends might process:

Financial reports (text data)

Stock price movements (numerical data)

CEO interviews (video and audio data)

By integrating these different modalities into a **knowledge graph**, the AI system can correlate data points more effectively and **generate richer insights**.

Example: Creating a Multimodal Knowledge Graph for Financial News Analysis

```
CREATE (:Company {name: "Tesla"})
CREATE (:Event {name: "Earnings Call"})
CREATE (:StockTrend {pattern: "Bullish"})
CREATE (:Transcript {content: "Our revenue grew by
20%"})
```

```
MATCH (c:Company {name: "Tesla"}), (e:Event {name:
"Earnings Call"}), (s:StockTrend {pattern:
"Bullish"}), (t:Transcript {content: "Our revenue
grew by 20%"})
CREATE (c)-[:HOSTED]->(e)
CREATE (e)-[:IMPACTED]->(s)
CREATE (e)-[:CONTAINS_TEXT]->(t)
```

A multimodal AI system analyzing this knowledge graph could **process video transcripts, stock price fluctuations, and CEO statements simultaneously**, ensuring that investment recommendations are **data-driven rather than purely speculative**.

Real-World Multimodal AI Applications

Amazon uses multimodal AI in **Alexa's voice assistant**, where the system processes **speech, text, and knowledge graphs** to generate contextual responses.

Google's **MUM (Multitask Unified Model)** integrates **image and text search**, allowing users to ask complex questions like **"Find hiking trails that look similar to this mountain picture"**—a task that traditional models struggle with.

Hybrid AI: Combining Deep Learning with Symbolic Reasoning

Deep learning excels at **pattern recognition**, but it struggles with **logical reasoning, causality, and explainability**. On the other hand, symbolic AI, which relies on predefined rules and structured knowledge, is **interpretable but lacks adaptability**.

The future of AI lies in **hybrid models that combine the strengths of deep learning and knowledge graphs**.

How Hybrid AI Works with Knowledge Graphs

A hybrid AI system might use **deep learning** for **perception tasks** (such as speech and image recognition) while relying on a **knowledge graph for structured reasoning and decision-making**.

For example, in **legal AI**, a system analyzing court cases can:

Use **natural language processing (NLP) models** to extract key points from legal documents.

Use a **knowledge graph** to check **case law precedents, statutes, and legal principles**.

Example: Hybrid AI for Legal Document Analysis

```
CREATE (:Law {name: "Consumer Protection Act"})
CREATE (:Case {name: "Consumer vs Corporation"})
CREATE (:Ruling {outcome: "Fine Imposed"})

MATCH (l:Law {name: "Consumer Protection Act"}),
(c:Case {name: "Consumer vs Corporation"}),
(r:Ruling {outcome: "Fine Imposed"})
CREATE (c)-[:CITED]->(l)
CREATE (c)-[:RESULTED_IN]->(r)
```

An AI assistant analyzing a new **legal dispute** can query this knowledge graph and provide lawyers with **relevant case precedents, legal interpretations, and recommended courses of action**.

Real-World Applications of Hybrid AI

IBM Watson uses **hybrid AI** in healthcare to analyze **radiology scans with deep learning** while referencing **medical knowledge graphs** to suggest diagnoses.

Self-driving cars use hybrid AI, where **neural networks detect obstacles**, while **symbolic AI ensures compliance with traffic laws**.

The future of AI will not be limited to **one dominant paradigm**. Instead, breakthroughs will come from integrating **federated learning for privacy, multimodal AI for richer understanding, and hybrid AI for explainability and reasoning**.

Knowledge graphs serve as the **unifying framework**, allowing AI systems to **process decentralized data, reason across multiple modalities, and bridge the gap between machine learning and structured decision-making**. As AI continues evolving, these emerging trends will shape **smarter, more ethical, and human-like AI systems**.

Next Decade of AI-Driven Knowledge Systems

Artificial intelligence has made significant progress in recent years, with models becoming more capable of processing text, images, and structured data. However, AI still faces fundamental challenges in **reasoning, memory retention, adaptability, and trustworthiness**. As we look toward the next decade, knowledge systems will play a crucial role in shaping AI into something more than just a predictive tool—they will make AI **context-aware, explainable, and capable of learning dynamically over time**.

Knowledge systems refer to AI models that **organize, store, and reason over structured information**, allowing them to **make decisions based on facts rather than just statistical correlations**. These systems will evolve rapidly, driven by advancements in **knowledge graphs, automated reasoning, federated learning, multimodal AI, and hybrid approaches that combine deep learning with symbolic reasoning**.

The next ten years will see AI-powered knowledge systems becoming **more scalable, interpretable, and useful across industries**, from **medicine and finance to cybersecurity and autonomous decision-making**.

Knowledge Graphs as the Foundation of AI Reasoning

One of the main limitations of today's AI models, including **large language models (LLMs) like GPT-4 and BERT**, is that they lack **structured memory and logical reasoning capabilities**. These models generate responses based on patterns in training data, but they do not **store or retrieve knowledge in a structured way**.

A **knowledge graph** addresses this issue by providing AI with a **persistent, structured way to represent entities and their relationships**.

For example, instead of treating "Paris is the capital of France" as just another sentence in a dataset, a knowledge graph would store it as:

Entity: Paris

Entity: France

Relationship: Paris **is the capital of** France

This allows an AI system to retrieve factual knowledge efficiently, understand context, and **build upon past information**.

Over the next decade, **knowledge graphs will become deeply integrated with AI models**, improving their ability to:

Retrieve **accurate and up-to-date information** in real-time

Provide **explainable decision-making** by tracing how a conclusion was reached

Adapt to **new facts dynamically**, rather than being frozen at the time of training

For instance, in **medical research**, AI-powered knowledge graphs can continuously update themselves with **new clinical trial results, drug interactions, and disease treatments**, ensuring that healthcare professionals always work with **the most relevant data**.

Automated Reasoning and the Evolution of AI Decision-Making

Today's AI models can recognize patterns, classify data, and generate text, but they struggle with **logical reasoning, causal inference, and knowledge synthesis**.

The next wave of AI-driven knowledge systems will incorporate **automated reasoning**, which enables AI to **infer new knowledge from existing facts**.

For example, an AI system designed for **cybersecurity** could detect a **previously unknown attack pattern** by reasoning over historical threat data. If a new malware strain shares **behavioral similarities** with past ransomware attacks, the AI can predict its likely impact, even if it has never seen this exact malware before.

Example: Knowledge Graph for Threat Intelligence Reasoning

```
CREATE (:Malware {name: "NewMalwareX"})
CREATE (:AttackVector {name: "Phishing Email"})
```

```
CREATE (:Exploit {name: "Zero-Day Vulnerability"})

MATCH (m:Malware {name: "NewMalwareX"}),
(a:AttackVector {name: "Phishing Email"}),
(e:Exploit {name: "Zero-Day Vulnerability"})
CREATE (m)-[:SPREADS_VIA]->(a)
CREATE (m)-[:USES]->(e)
```

An AI system querying this knowledge graph can **identify relationships between attack methods and vulnerabilities**, helping cybersecurity teams **predict potential threats before they escalate**.

As AI reasoning improves, **knowledge-based AI will shift from merely detecting patterns to actively solving complex problems in real-time**.

The Rise of Multimodal Knowledge Systems

Most AI models today specialize in **either text, images, or numerical data**, but they do not integrate multiple types of information effectively. The future of AI will be **multimodal**, meaning that AI systems will be able to **process and reason across text, images, video, speech, and structured data simultaneously**.

For example, an **AI-powered legal assistant** will need to:

Analyze **contracts (text-based legal documents)**

Understand **courtroom transcripts (speech-to-text conversion)**

Process **case law and legal precedents (structured knowledge graphs)**

A multimodal AI system could **combine all these elements** to provide a comprehensive legal recommendation.

Example: Integrating Legal Knowledge with AI Reasoning

```
CREATE (:LegalCase {name: "Privacy Violation
Lawsuit"})
CREATE (:Law {name: "Data Protection Act"})
CREATE (:Evidence {type: "Email Leak", severity:
"High"})
```

```
MATCH (c:LegalCase {name: "Privacy Violation
Lawsuit"}), (l:Law {name: "Data Protection Act"}),
(e:Evidence {type: "Email Leak"})
CREATE (c)-[:CITED]->(l)
CREATE (c)-[:CONTAINS_EVIDENCE]->(e)
```

A **multimodal AI legal assistant** could analyze a lawsuit by linking:

Text from legal documents

Audio from court proceedings

Structured legal precedents from a knowledge graph

By integrating these sources, AI can **provide case predictions, summarize legal arguments, and recommend actions for lawyers**, making legal decision-making more efficient.

Federated Learning for Secure and Distributed Knowledge Sharing

One of the biggest challenges for AI-driven knowledge systems is **data privacy and security**. Organizations often deal with **sensitive information** that cannot be centralized due to regulatory constraints (e.g., healthcare patient records, financial transactions, classified government data).

The next decade will see **federated learning and distributed knowledge graphs** becoming the standard for **privacy-preserving AI**.

Instead of collecting all data into a single location, **federated learning allows AI models to learn across multiple institutions without exposing raw data**.

For example, a network of hospitals could train a shared AI model to detect **early-stage cancer patterns** without ever sharing patient data across locations.

Example: Federated Learning with a Distributed Medical Knowledge Graph

```
CREATE (:Hospital {name: "Mayo Clinic"})
CREATE (:Hospital {name: "Cleveland Clinic"})
CREATE (:Disease {name: "Pancreatic Cancer"})
```

```
CREATE (:ResearchFinding {summary: "New Biomarker
Discovered"})

MATCH (h1:Hospital {name: "Mayo Clinic"}),
(h2:Hospital {name: "Cleveland Clinic"}),
(d:Disease {name: "Pancreatic Cancer"}),
(r:ResearchFinding {summary: "New Biomarker
Discovered"})
CREATE (h1)-[:STUDYING]->(d)
CREATE (h2)-[:STUDYING]->(d)
CREATE (d)-[:LINKED_TO]->(r)
```

Each hospital updates its local knowledge graph, and federated learning **allows AI models to benefit from shared insights without violating privacy laws**.

As this approach gains traction, **privacy-preserving AI will become the standard for healthcare, finance, and defense applications**.

Over the next decade, AI-driven knowledge systems will **fundamentally reshape how machines reason, learn, and interact with data**. By integrating **knowledge graphs, automated reasoning, multimodal AI, and federated learning**, AI models will become **more accurate, explainable, and adaptive**.

These advancements will lead to **real-time decision-making AI in healthcare, finance, cybersecurity, and legal systems**, ensuring that AI is not just generating outputs but **providing logical, trustworthy, and fact-based conclusions**.

The combination of **structured knowledge and deep learning** will be the key to unlocking **AI systems that can understand, adapt, and solve complex problems autonomously**—pushing artificial intelligence closer to **true general intelligence**.

Conclusion

Artificial intelligence has reached a turning point where models are no longer limited to statistical pattern recognition. The integration of structured knowledge, reasoning, and dynamic learning has transformed AI from a tool that generates predictions into a system capable of understanding, adapting, and explaining its decisions. Throughout this book, the role of knowledge graphs in shaping the next generation of AI has been explored, from their fundamental structure to their applications in reasoning, decision-making, and enterprise solutions.

AI's effectiveness depends not just on its ability to process vast amounts of data but on its capability to **organize, retrieve, and infer meaningful insights from that data in a structured way**. Traditional machine learning models, including large language models, struggle with contextual consistency, factual accuracy, and long-term memory. Knowledge graphs address these limitations by providing AI with a **framework for structured relationships, contextual understanding, and logical inference**.

The progress in AI-driven knowledge systems is not just a technical evolution—it is a transformation in how AI interacts with the world around it. The ability to represent knowledge dynamically, update information in real-time, and reason over complex datasets is essential for AI to function as a reliable assistant, advisor, and decision-maker. This shift from raw data processing to **knowledge-driven AI** will redefine industries, enabling machines to **think, explain, and refine their understanding over time**.

As AI models become more deeply integrated into critical fields such as healthcare, finance, cybersecurity, and legal analysis, the demand for transparency, accountability, and reliability continues to grow. Knowledge graphs, combined with advancements in automated reasoning, multimodal AI, and federated learning, provide the foundation for AI systems that are not only powerful but also explainable and trustworthy.

Looking ahead, AI will move beyond its current capabilities by incorporating more **adaptive, federated, and multimodal approaches**. Systems will no longer operate in isolation but will collaborate across distributed networks while maintaining privacy and security. Machines will learn from structured and unstructured data simultaneously, drawing insights from text, images, videos, and structured databases in a way that mimics human cognition.

The goal is no longer just to create AI that can generate responses but to build AI that **understands, reasons, and continuously improves its knowledge base**. Knowledge graphs are at the core of this transformation, ensuring that AI does not simply memorize information but learns how to connect, interpret, and apply knowledge meaningfully.

The next decade will see AI-driven knowledge systems becoming an integral part of human decision-making, enabling AI to act as a collaborative partner rather than just a computational tool. With structured knowledge guiding AI's learning process, the future of artificial intelligence will be defined by **precision, adaptability, and depth of understanding**. AI will not only answer questions but will explain its reasoning, validate its conclusions, and refine its insights, making it a more effective and responsible part of human progress.